A Resource for Schools (K-12)

D1551114

Coping with Crisis

A Quick Reference

Scott Poland and Jami S. McCormick

Copyright 2000 by Sopris West
All rights reserved.

07 06 05 04 03   7 6 5 4 3

No portion of this booklet, in whole or in part, may be reprinted by any means, electronic or otherwise, without the express written permission of the publisher.

Permission is granted to the purchasing school/agency/individual to photocopy small numbers of the pages of this booklet for parent, teacher, and/or volunteer use within the affected school/community only. However, each member of the crisis response team should be provided his or her own copy of this inexpensive resource. Photocopied pages may not be utilized in any other published work or for-profit training without the express written permission of the publisher.

Neither the publisher nor the authors assume any liability for the use or misuse of the strategies described in this booklet. Nothing in this booklet is intended as a substitute for trained police, medical, or other professional intervention when warranted.

Proofreading by Beverly Rokes
Cover and Layout Design by Becky Malone
Cover Images © 2000 PhotoDisc, Inc.

ISBN 1-57035-269-0

Printed in the United States of America

Published and Distributed by

SOPRIS
WEST
EDUCATIONAL SERVICES

4093 Specialty Place • Longmont, Colorado 80504 • (303) 651-2829
www.sopriswest.com

108PERT/1-03/KEN/1.25M/2.29

dedication

To the healing communities of West Paducah, Kentucky, Jonesboro, Arkansas, and Littleton, Colorado, and to all other school communities that have been so tragically affected by youth violence and other crises. It is our hope that the lessons learned from those tragedies will assist others in coping with school crises in the future.

about the authors

Scott Poland, Ed.D., is director of Psychological Services for the Cypress-Fairbanks Independent School District in Houston, Texas. He is a former chair and current member of the National Association of School Psychologists (NASP) emergency team, and was chosen to serve as president of NASP during the 1999-2000 and 2000-2001 school years. Dr. Poland was selected as a member of the U.S. Department of Education assistance team that advised the superintendent of the Oklahoma City schools in the aftermath of the 1995 bombing of the Alfred P. Murrah Federal Building. He was the team leader for the National Organization for Victim Assistance (NOVA) teams that responded to the school shootings in West Paducah, Kentucky, and near Jonesboro, Arkansas, and in 1999 he provided onsite assistance to schools in Littleton, Colorado, after the shooting at Columbine High School. He also led US Department of Education violence response teams after school shootings in El Cajon and Santee, California. He has written numerous books, book chapters, and articles on school crisis intervention. In 1998, 1999, and 2001, he provided congressional testimony on violent children to the Early Childhood, Youth and Families Subcommittee of the United States House of Representatives Education and the Workforce Committee and in 1998 participated in the President's Roundtable on Youth Violence. In May 1999, Dr. Poland assisted Vice President Al Gore in leading discussions concerning school violence in Dallas, Texas, schools. He is a recipient of the Houston Wage Peace Award and was chosen as the outstanding psychologist in Texas for 2001. He provided extensive consultation and training to school personnel following 9/11/01. Dr. Poland has provided school crisis training in locations as diverse as Turkey and China.

Jami S. McCormick is a professional writer specializing in education issues (K-12) and youth violence. Formerly the senior editor of an educational publishing house, her business—Tapestry Publishing Services of Louisville, Colorado—provides writing, editing, book proposal consultation, and Web site content services to independent writers, publishers, and corporations. She has served on the board of directors of TEENS, Inc., a Colorado youth development/violence prevention organization, and is a member of Mothers Against Violence in America.

contents

continued—

References

For a complete list of the sources that contributed to the checklists in this booklet, see the References at the end of each corresponding chapter of Coping With Crisis: Lessons Learned.

introduction

How to Use This Booklet

This booklet is for use by school crisis responders and school staff members during and after a severe school crisis. We define a severe school crisis as any situation in which a school community member is seriously injured or is killed (whether accidentally or as the result of violence, such as a student fight or school shooting) or any situation in the surrounding community that negatively impacts a school (e.g., a natural disaster or unsolved crime). When such events occur, a school usually requires a number of days (and sometimes weeks, months, or even years) to regain its equilibrium.

The checklists in this booklet summarize the detailed recommendations contained in our book *Coping With Crisis: Lessons Learned* (Poland & McCormick, 1999) and you are encouraged to consult that resource for a full explanation of any or all of the points. (The checklists contained herein are presented in roughly the same sequence as the material in the main book.) Using the two resources together will be particularly helpful for crisis response planning and team member training. In the midst of an actual crisis, however, you will likely not have the time to read the chapters of the book. That's when this booklet will be invaluable: It tells you exactly *what you need to know* and *what you need to do, right now*, to assist your school community to weather any sort of crisis. These sequential checklists provide an easy-to-follow, comprehensive plan for a timely and effective crisis response. Note that these recommended actions will complement any existing crisis response plan; even schools with an existing plan will benefit from the use of this booklet.

One or two people alone cannot provide all the help needed in mitigating the effects of a severe school crisis on students, school staff, their families, and the community as a whole. The school administrator will need a team of people to help address the various aspects of the crisis, ranging from media relations to counseling students. In the best-case scenario, your school or district will have an organized and trained crisis response team ready to respond to a severe school crisis. When a crisis strikes in a school without such a team in place, however, an impromptu team must be quickly organized. Fortunately, members of the school community who can remain relatively calm in a crisis and can assume a leadership role will immediately emerge. These people will ideally be the school administrators, counselors and school psychologists, the

school nurse (if you have one), and security staff/peace officers/constables (if applicable); they may also include members of the teaching and support staffs. The primary roles these people will need to fill are the following:

- **Crisis Coordinator.** The Crisis Coordinator is preferably the head administrator of your school. Another option is for the administrator and a school psychologist to co-coordinate the crisis response team (Lieberman, 1999). Either way, it is the head administrator of the affected school, as opposed to the superintendent or someone else from the central office, who should lead or co-lead the crisis intervention effort. This person (or persons) will coordinate the crisis intervention and remain available and visible to the school community. He or she must be steady by nature, a leader who is able to calm and empower others. In addition, he or she should be an orderly and clear thinker and someone who is able to delegate efficiently.

- **Medical Liaison.** If your school has a nurse, he or she is the logical person to fill this role. This person (or persons) will administer first aid, triage the injured, keep a record of who is injured and where they are transported (and communicate this information to the Parent/Family Liaison), and serve as a liaison between the school and hospital personnel.

- **Security Liaison.** If your school has a security officer, constable, or peace officer, he or she is the appropriate person to fill this role. This person (or persons) will secure the crime scene and evidence until the police arrive, if applicable. He or she will also limit access to the campus by the media and, if necessary, help to dissuade those who insist upon volunteering their assistance to your school.

- **Media Liaison.** If your school (or district) has a public information/public relations representative, he or she is the logical person to fill this role. This person must be authoritative yet sympathetic and preferably have training in public speaking. He or she will hold press conferences and keep the media updated as the crisis unfolds. Note, however, that at some point in a severe crisis the press will want to hear from the head administrator of your school (and likely the superintendent, as well). If the Media Liaison is not also the head administrator, he or she can help prepare the administrator for the press conference(s)/interview(s).

- **Parent/Family Liaison.** This person (or persons) will provide parents and other family members with verbal and written information about the crisis and make sure the information communicated to them is consistent. (The Parent/Family Liaison will delegate part of this task to the school secretaries/receptionists who answer the phones for your school.) The Parent/Family Liaison will address parents and other family members when they arrive at the school, deliver injury/death/missing notifications, and plan the family/community meeting(s). Because this is a sensitive assignment, a member of your school's counseling staff or an administrator would be an ideal person to fill this role.

- **Counseling Liaison.** The school psychologist, counselor, or social worker is the obvious person to fill the role of Counseling Liaison. This person (or persons) will work to calm students, staff, and family members during the crisis. He or she also will provide counseling sessions (both small group and individual) for students and staff after the crisis and advocate for opportunities for staff and students to express their emotions.

- **Campus Liaison.** This person (or persons) will communicate the specifics of the crisis to the school staff (both faculty and support staff), give the staff guidance on how they can assist in the crisis management, and allow them opportunities to express their emotions about the crisis. The Campus Liaison will also greet and briefly "interview" any volunteers (e.g., mental health practitioners) who come to your school to assist with the crisis response, assign any authorized helpers their tasks for the day, and coordinate their activities. Further, he or she will help to evaluate the scope of the crisis and the need for outside assistance and will discuss this need with the Crisis Coordinator. A member of your school's counseling staff or an administrator is the logical person to fill this role.

Within the first ten to 15 minutes of a severe school crisis, the highest-ranking administrator of your school who is present at the time should assign one or more people to each of these crisis response roles. This task should not require an inordinate amount of discussion, nor should school bureaucracy or politics play a part. The administrator should simply find out what each person feels most comfortable handling, take a few minutes to make sure everyone is clear about who is doing what, put a copy of this booklet into the hands of each crisis responder, and then jump into action.

Throughout this booklet it is assumed that your crisis response team members will generally fill the roles as outlined above. For example, the Media Liaison would likely hold press conferences, and thus would be the person carrying out the recommendations in the media section. The Counseling Liaison would likely coordinate counseling sessions for students and staff; thus the section on providing counseling services is written with that person in mind. And so forth. For added clarity, the specific people recommended to take the necessary actions are listed at the beginning of each checklist. A quick reference key for these actions is also provided at the end of this booklet. Note, however, that these specifications are merely *guidelines*. By nature, crisis response is chaotic and fluid, and it is often beneficial to set aside rigid perceptions of workplace responsibilities and relationships. It is more important that the tasks we identify be addressed than who, exactly, will address them.

Another important consideration is delegation. Each of the team member roles is labor-intensive, and at times it may be physically impossible for a single individual to fulfill all aspects of a particular role. For example, the Parent/Family Liaison cannot be both meeting parents at the main entrance of the school and delivering injury/death/missing notifications privately to family members. In such cases, the team member will need the assistance of additional school staff or authorized volunteers. For simplicity, we have not specified each instance when "assistants" may be useful. Each crisis situation is different, and the key is for all concerned to ask for the help they need. Team members are encouraged to grab any available staff member and delegate with efficiency.

We have *not* specified the involvement of emergency responders (e.g., police officers, paramedics/EMTs, firefighters) and the various outside agencies/organizations that might be involved in the crisis response (such as the Red Cross, National Guard, or victims' advocates), for two reasons. First, each crisis situation varies dramatically from any other, and attempting to outline every possible scenario in which these people could assist your school would be far too cumbersome. Second, and most important, these trained professionals have their own procedures to follow in responding to a crisis and will not need, or likely welcome, direction from the school. Likewise, any specially trained crisis response team (e.g., a NOVA or NEAT team—*see Section Four*) lending their expertise to your school will already be familiar with the principles of this proven response plan. Thus, the roles for members of outside agencies/organizations and crisis response teams are not specified.

References

Lieberman, R. (1999, January 22-23). *Crisis Intervention Workshop*, Walnut Creek, California.

Poland, S. & McCormick, J. S. (1999). *Coping with crisis: Lessons learned*. Longmont, CO: Sopris West.

section **one**

When a Crisis Strikes

This section covers the recommended actions to be initiated in the first hour of a severe school crisis. The actions taken—or not taken—during the first hour will set the stage for the rest of the intervention and will, in large part, determine the degree of success of the overall crisis response. As discussed in the "Introduction" to this booklet, the head administrator of the affected school should first form an impromptu school-based crisis response team (if a team is not already in place). *There are then six main tasks for the team to get started in the first hour, the first two of which will need to happen immediately:*

1. Address human safety and provide medical assistance.

2. Summon help.

3. Secure the crime scene (if any) and contain the media.

4. Verify the facts and prepare a Crisis Fact Sheet.

5. Deliver injury/death/missing notifications.

6. Communicate the facts to parents/other family members.

The amount of material covered in this section may seem at first glance overwhelming, but it is the lion's share of the crisis response. Your crisis response team will likely continue to work on some of these tasks throughout the first day of the crisis. The point is that these are the actions that must be initiated right away.

Forming an Impromptu Crisis Response Team

What You Need to KNOW

- One person cannot address all the aspects of a severe crisis: A team response is needed.

- Do not let politics or your school's hierarchy get in the way of making these assignments quickly. Natural leaders will emerge in the face of a crisis. Use these people!

What You Need to DO

Who Should Do It: ✔ Head administrator of affected school

❑ Quickly assign one or more people to fill each of the following roles:
(1) Crisis Coordinator (and backup), (2) Medical Liaison, (3) Security Liaison,
(4) Media Liaison, (5) Parent/Family Liaison, (6) Counseling Liaison, and
(7) Campus Liaison. (*See the "Introduction" to this booklet for team member
"job descriptions."*)

Disarming a Perpetrator

What You Need to KNOW

- You are not legally required to jeopardize your own safety by physically
intervening.

- Only you can determine your own reaction if you find yourself near an
armed assailant.

- Verbal intervention is safer than physical intervention.

What You Need to DO

Who Should Do It: ✔ Any school community member

❑ Send a responsible student or a staff member to the front office for help immediately.

❑ If possible, have an adult whom the aggressor likes or respects (e.g., a favorite
teacher) intervene.

Triage/First Aid

What You Need to KNOW

- Any staff members (or onlookers gathered at the scene) with first aid training
can assist the school nurse/Medical Liaison. Ask for their help over the intercom, if
necessary.

- Cardiopulmonary resuscitation (CPR) is best performed by someone trained in this
procedure. But if no such person is available, and a victim is not breathing, a staff
member should still begin CPR. *Do not give chest compressions if there is a heartbeat—
doing so may cause the heart to stop beating!*

- Do not delay in providing immediate medical attention to seriously wounded
students, whether or not their parents can be reached.

- Do not move victims unless they are in immediate danger.

- Do not move victims in any way if there is suspicion of a spinal injury (i.e., weakness/numbness in an extremity, inability to move an extremity, or lack of feeling in an extremity).

What You Need to DO

Who Should Do It: ✔ Medical Liaison
✔ Any school community member with first aid training

❑ Send a responsible student or another staff member to the front office and nurse's office for help immediately.

❑ Do everything possible and appropriate to assist victims until an ambulance arrives.

❑ Keep victims warm, and reassure them that they will be okay.

❑ Identify the victims, and put an identification wristband on each victim or write their names on their hands in ink.

❑ Do not give victims anything to eat or drink or any medicines.

❑ Do not use a tourniquet unless blood loss is so severe and rapid as to be immediately life threatening. Note the time when a tourniquet is applied.

❑ List those injured and/or killed, and photocopy this list for the Parent/Family Liaison.

❑ If the victims are students, pull their emergency notification forms in the front office. Photocopy these forms for use by both the Medical Liaison and Parent/Family Liaison.

Protecting Students and Staff

What You Need to KNOW

- If shots are fired, running can make you a target. Crawling to safety is safer.
- The police may talk to student witnesses without their parents or a counselor present.

What You Need to DO

Who Should Do It: ✔ Any school community member in danger
✔ Counseling Liaison

❑ If gunshots are fired, drop and roll. Remain on the ground or beneath a desk with your hands covering your head.

❑ Follow your school's predetermined emergency plan and any instructions from the Crisis Coordinator/head administrator.

continued—

❑ *See "Less Severe Crises" in Chapter One of the main* Coping With Crisis *book for step-by-step procedures to follow in the event of student fights, a threatening person outside the building, an armed intruder inside the building, or a bomb threat.*

❑ After the crisis incident, staff should get all those who do not need medical attention back to their classrooms as quickly as possible (as soon as it is safe for students/staff to move). The Counseling Liaison can coordinate this effort.

❑ If there are numerous witnesses to the incident, send them back to their classrooms for the time being.

❑ If there are only a few witnesses to the incident, have them wait for the police in the front office or counselor's office.

❑ Comfort these witnesses; however, do not counsel them before they've talked with the police.

Summoning Police/Medical Personnel

What You Need to KNOW

• No matter what your school's hierarchy is, when emergency responders must be summoned, the first person who can get to a phone—including a student—should call 911.

• Call for emergency responder assistance before calling anyone else (e.g., the central office).

What You Need to DO

Who Should Do It: ✔ Any school community member
✔ Crisis Coordinator/head administrator of affected school
✔ Medical Liaison

❑ Call for emergency services first—dial 911 or 0.

❑ Do not hang up until directed to do so by the emergency operator.

❑ Post someone outside your school to flag down emergency crews and direct them to the scene.

❑ The Medical Liaison (and others, if necessary) should accompany the wounded to the hospital—one staff member per ambulance. Drive carefully if you travel in your own car!

❑ Bring a copy of the pertinent emergency notification forms and the list of those injured and/or killed.

❑ Keep the school—particularly the Parent/Family Liaison—updated on the status of the injured by calling from the hospital. Also be sure the school knows to which hospital(s) the victims were taken.

Alerting the Central Office

What You Need to KNOW

- An administrator of the affected school, rather than a central office representative, should publicly lead (or co-lead) the crisis intervention.

- However, it is critical for the school system's top leader to go to the school in crisis immediately to lend support.

What You Need to DO

Who Should Do It: ✔ Crisis Coordinator/highest-ranking administrator of affected school who is present

❑ Call the central office to alert the superintendent and other district staff (including any preestablished crisis team members) of the crisis.

❑ Call any school administrators and school leaders (e.g., school psychologist) who are away from the building.

Notifying Area Schools

What You Need to KNOW

- Use e-mail, "walkie-talkies," or any other method available that is faster than the phone.

- In a citywide crisis, or one in which multiple schools are directly affected, the principals should communicate as quickly as possible to coordinate their crisis responses.

What You Need to DO

Who Should Do It: ✔ Central office staff

❑ Quickly alert nearby schools of the severe crisis so they can protect their students and staff.

❑ Begin with those schools closest to the school in crisis, for safety reasons. Then contact any schools at which you know there are family members of victims/potential victims, and feeder schools.

❑ Alert both the administration and counseling staff at those schools.

❑ Share the facts with all schools in the district, as others may also have family members and friends of victims/potential victims anxious for news.

Securing the Crime Scene and Containing the Media

What You Need to KNOW

- When the police arrive, they are in charge of the situation.
- No one should call the media! They will probably find out about the crisis on their own and the later that they arrive on the scene the better. Their presence in the first hour will not be helpful to your school.
- The media may arrive as quickly as (or even before) emergency response personnel. It is important to contain the media outside the school (preferably off the school grounds).

What You Need to DO

Who Should Do It: ✔ Security Liaison

❑ Without impeding the movements of medical caregivers, secure the area.

❑ Do not allow anyone to handle anything that could be considered physical evidence (if a crime has been committed).

❑ Immediately send a staff member outside to control the flow of traffic in front of and around the school. It is essential that vehicles of family members and media representatives do not block emergency vehicles' access.

❑ Verbally refuse access to the campus by the media. If your state does not have a law entitling you to do so, simply run a bluff! Assume the authority, and don't back down.

❑ Ask for police assistance in containing the media, if necessary. Do not get physical with media representatives.

Getting/Verifying the Facts

What You Need to KNOW

- Any crisis information communicated must be accurate and as complete as possible.
- Your school's head administrator/Crisis Coordinator and/or professional emergency responders (e.g., a police officer) must verify all information before it is disseminated.

What You Need to DO

Who Should Do It: ✔ All crisis response team members
✔ Crisis Coordinator/head administrator of affected school
✔ Counseling Liaison (and/or Parent/Family Liaison)

❑ No crisis response team member or staff member should provide unconfirmed information. Say, "I don't know," "We'll let you know when we know more ourselves," or "You need to ask (the Crisis Coordinator) for that information."

❑ If the incident happened during off-school hours, obtain the facts directly from the police and/or the families of the school community members affected.

❑ The Crisis Coordinator and Counseling Liaison (and/or the Parent/Family Liaison or another school counselor or psychologist) should contact the families of victims in person. This first contact with family members of injured/deceased/missing school community members is important: Handle the meetings with delicacy and diplomacy.

Telling the Facts

What You Need to KNOW

- A Crisis Fact Sheet is a written statement used to communicate crisis information to everyone concerned (i.e., staff and students, parents and other family members, the media, and community members). (*For a sample Crisis Fact Sheet, see "Verifying Information/Crisis Fact Sheet" in Chapter One of the main* Coping With Crisis *book.*)

- Although it may seem impossible immediately after a crisis to take the time to put anything down in writing, it is important to make the time. Spending ten to 15 minutes in the first hour to create a Crisis Fact Sheet is crucial to consistently communicating about the incident during the rest of the crisis response.

- If your school or community includes people for whom English is a second language or includes a bilingual population, remember to produce the Crisis Fact Sheet in all relevant languages.

- Do not deviate from the information contained on your Crisis Fact Sheet. Doing so will likely create a serious public relations headache.

- No matter how bad the facts are, the rumors that will spread if those facts are not disseminated will be worse! Tell the *whole truth*. (This may require courage, but you cannot withhold information.)

- All members of the school community—*including students, even young students*—must be given the facts. Use age-appropriate vocabulary and a quiet, direct manner.

- Be as factually complete and accurate as possible. Receiving the correct information will be very important to family members and friends of victims. *continued—*

What You Need to DO

Who Should Do It:
- ✔ Crisis Coordinator/head administrator of affected school
- ✔ Media Liaison
- ✔ Parent/Family Liaison
- ✔ Central office staff (superintendent or designee)
- ✔ Campus Liaison
- ✔ Teachers and/or Counseling Liaison

❑ As quickly as possible, create a Crisis Fact Sheet. Include only verified, accurate information. Be as thorough as possible. Express your concern, but also be positive about your school's crisis response.

❑ Write the Crisis Fact Sheet as a group. At a minimum, the Crisis Coordinator, Media Liaison, and Parent/Family Liaison should collaborate on its content. The Crisis Coordinator/head administrator must sign off on its content, and your superintendent or designee may also need to approve this statement before it is distributed.

❑ Include on the Crisis Fact Sheet all known facts about what happened; the status of victims and suspected perpetrator(s); whether the school will remain open the rest of the day and if parents are encouraged to leave their children in school; and information about the counseling services being made available.

❑ Also include on the Crisis Fact Sheet the time/location of the family/community meeting to be held the evening of the crisis. Don't worry if you don't yet know what you will say at that meeting—you need to have it, and you need to publicize it. (*See "Why to Hold a Family/Community Meeting" and related points in Section Two of this booklet for more information.*)

❑ As soon as the Crisis Fact Sheet is finalized, clear the photocopy machine and assign someone to reproduce this statement. You'll need many copies on hand when parents and others begin arriving at your school.

❑ Send a staff member to the hospital with copies of the Crisis Fact Sheet for the Medical Liaison.

❑ Tell *everything* that has been confirmed to *everybody* concerned.

❑ Tell everything you know as soon as it is verified as accurate. Continue to share known facts as they are updated throughout the day, including updating and redistributing the Crisis Fact Sheet.

❑ If a crisis occurs outside of school hours, notify the staff while they are still at home using your prearranged calling tree. Invite all the faculty and support staff to a meeting before school to fully explain the loss/crisis and to discuss ways to assist the students with the crisis situation. (During this meeting the Campus Liaison will communicate crisis response instructions and allow staff members to vent their emotions and ask questions.)

❏ If a calling tree is not an option, provide for backup coverage to begin the day in classes of affected staff members. Additionally, put a written statement regarding the crisis (to include the Crisis Fact Sheet) in all staff mailboxes in the morning. The Campus Liaison should be nearby to answer staff questions.

❏ Unless doing so is impossible, share the crisis information with students in their classroom/homeroom. Never group multiple classes (or gather the entire student body) together to share the facts. Depending upon the severity of the crisis, teachers can read a prepared statement to their classes or an administrator and member of the counseling staff (e.g., the Counseling Liaison) can visit each affected classroom.

❏ Answer questions honestly, but offer as few details as possible. In particular, avoid grisly or unnecessary details.

❏ Avoid religious symbolism and platitudes.

❏ Encourage the expression of natural human emotions and feelings about the crisis.

❏ Share crisis facts via the intercom only when information must be immediately disseminated (i.e., there is no time to alert the staff/students on a class-by-class basis). The Crisis Coordinator should deliver any statement made over the intercom. Voice tone and inflection are very important. Choose your words carefully and rehearse your delivery. The best method is to read word-for-word from a prepared statement.

❏ Do not release the names of victims to anyone outside the school they attend(ed)/work(ed) in before their families have been notified.

❏ Before sharing sensitive information, consider what information the police, families, and/or the media have and have not already released. In appropriate cases you should say, "That information is not available at this time."

❏ Do not release any photos of the injured or deceased without permission from the parents/family members.

Delivering Injury, Death, and Missing Notifications

What You Need to KNOW

- You are giving a death notification any time you are the first person to tell another that someone he or she knows has died—whether you do so in person or on the telephone.

- Affected family members should be given injury/death notification when school personnel are certain about what happened. If the facts are known, family members should not be kept in suspense. Don't cop out by saying, "It's serious, it's bad, we don't know."

- Extreme care must be taken to avoid notifying someone of a death prematurely or mistakenly! Deliver a death notification only when a school community member is pronounced dead on the scene by a professional emergency responder (i.e., *continued—*

a paramedic/EMT, a police officer, a firefighter) or by the coroner's office, and only when you've heard this information firsthand. If it is uncertain whether a victim will survive, give the family members injury notification but allow the death notification (if necessary) to be handled at the hospital.

- When you mention someone's death, you may not know that you are giving a death notification, and it is important to be sensitive to this fact. Not only family members but also close friends, colleagues, and even acquaintances may react with strong emotions when they hear of a victim's injury or death.

- Death notification must be handled as well as possible, because it is the critical point of trauma for most survivors.

What You Need to DO

Who Should Do It: ✔ Parent/Family Liaison
                      ✔ Medical Liaison

❑ Attempt to make telephone contact with the appropriate family members as quickly as possible. (*For step-by-step instructions for giving an injury/death notification on the telephone, see "Injury/Death Notification" in Chapter One of the main* Coping With Crisis *book.*)

❑ In a severe crisis, panicked parents and other family members will likely arrive at the school within minutes of word of the crisis. Separate any family members of victims who arrive at the school, and quickly and privately deliver the necessary injury/death notification. (*For step-by-step instructions for giving an injury/death notification in person, see "Injury/Death Notification" in Chapter One of the main* Coping With Crisis *book.*)

❑ Some families may go directly to the hospital seeking information about their loved ones' whereabouts and condition. The Medical Liaison (and other staff members at the hospital to assist him or her) should facilitate necessary injury/death notifications and emotionally support surviving family members at that time. (*For step-by-step instructions for assisting in an injury/death notification at the hospital and for assisting in the viewing of bodies, see "Injury/Death Notification" in Chapter One of the main* Coping With Crisis *book.*)

❑ If a school community member is missing and believed to be a crisis victim, provide the family members with a "missing notification" as soon as possible. (*For step-by-step instructions for giving a missing notification, see "Injury/Death Notification" in Chapter One of the main* Coping With Crisis *book.*) If and when the status of the potential victim is clarified, follow up with any necessary injury/death notification immediately.

Communicating With Parents/Other Family Members

What You Need to KNOW

- Parents and other family members will naturally want to find out if their loved ones are safe and will telephone and come to the school in great numbers during a severe crisis.

- The school should proactively communicate with the families of any students or staff directly affected by the crisis.

What You Need to DO

Who Should Do It: ✔ Crisis Coordinator/head administrator of affected school
✔ Counseling Liaison
✔ School secretaries/receptionists
✔ Parent/Family Liaison

❑ Contact the parents of affected students—those who were victims; those who witnessed the crisis and were questioned by the police; students who may be especially traumatized by the crisis, such as close friends of victims or suspected student perpetrator(s); and the parents of suspected student perpetrator(s) (if applicable).

❑ Likewise, contact the family members of staff who were victims in the crisis.

❑ Use the same care and sensitivity when delivering news of the crisis to family members of suspected student perpetrator(s) as you would with victims' families. (These families may or may not have already been contacted by the police.)

❑ Provide the parents of affected students with information about typical childhood reactions to crisis and what they can do to assist their children (*see "Childhood/ Adolescent Crisis Reactions" in Section Seven of this booklet*).

❑ When family members call the school, the school secretaries/receptionists should tell everyone the same thing: the content of the Crisis Fact Sheet. Do not deviate from the Crisis Fact Sheet.

❑ Transfer family members calling for the medical status of their loved ones to the Parent/Family Liaison. The school secretaries/receptionists should not deliver injury/death/missing notifications.

❑ The Parent/Family Liaison should briefly (as time allows) document each such parental contact.

❑ Have all family members who arrive at the school seeking information gather in one place to hear the facts of the crisis and news of their loved ones. Post a staff member at the door to meet and direct parents and other family members to the specified gathering place.

continued—

❏ When family members arrive, have them sign in and ask them the name of the student/staff member to whom they are related. Any family member who needs to hear an injury/death/missing notification should immediately be accompanied to an adjacent room by the Parent/Family Liaison. (*See "Injury/Death Notification" in Chapter One of the main* Coping With Crisis *book for detailed instructions.*)

❏ If family members of suspected student perpetrator(s) arrive at the school, keep them separated from the other family members (particularly those of the victims). A school staff member should offer to drive them home or to the police station.

❏ Provide all of the family members with a copy of the Crisis Fact Sheet, and strongly encourage them to attend the family/community meeting to be held the evening of the crisis. (*See "Why to Hold a Family/Community Meeting" and related points in Section Two of this booklet for details about the meeting's format and content.*)

❏ If you are keeping the school open for the rest of the day (*see "First-Day Task List" in Section Two of this booklet*), encourage parents to leave their children in school, where they will receive the assistance of the staff. Parents will be more likely to do so if they see a calm, orderly, and safe crisis response taking place.

❏ Ask family members leaving the school to not speak with the media. Explain that school representatives want to do everything they can to ensure that the information released is accurate. Ask the family members to respect the privacy of other families and refrain from providing the names of, or information about, victims, suspected student perpetrator(s), and their families, if they do decide to talk with reporters.

section two

Continuing the Crisis Response

This section outlines the crisis response from the point where Section One left off, providing a "game plan" for the rest of the first day—and evening—of the severe school crisis. Note that during this time your crisis response team will likely need to continue to work on the tasks listed in Section One of this booklet as well as carry out the tasks described following. Thus, there is some overlap between these two sections.

First-Day Task List

What You Need to KNOW

- The first day of a severe crisis will be a very long one. As a member of the crisis response team, you will need to make whatever arrangements are necessary (e.g., childcare for your own children) in order to devote yourself solely to the crisis response well into the night.

- If a member of your team finds he or she cannot do the job for some reason, don't question or criticize the team member; quickly find a replacement.

- If your school will be closed for longer than 24 hours due to damage or an ongoing police investigation, it is important to quickly arrange for an alternate location or locations where your students can gather in classroom groups (e.g., a nearby school, community college/university campus building, a stadium/auditorium). Strive to return your students to school in some form on the day immediately following the crisis incident (or at least within a couple of days) so that they can receive the assistance of trained school personnel. Don't worry about being well organized; it's more important to provide students with the structure of meeting with their class and the opportunity to "process" their reactions to the crisis. Meanwhile, make every effort to reopen your campus as soon after the crisis as is possible.

continued—

- Very young students (e.g., kindergartners) should be reunited with their primary caretakers as soon as possible after a traumatic event. Older students should remain at school, if possible, as they will benefit from the assistance of trained school staff members in processing their crisis reactions.

- The Crisis Fact Sheet should be updated as new facts are verified.

- If your school or community includes people for whom English is a second language or includes a bilingual population, remember to produce all written information for parents (such as the parent/family information packet and parent letter) in all relevant languages.

- *If the crisis involved the suicide of a school community member, see Section Eleven of this booklet, "Special Considerations for Suicide," for postvention guidelines.*

What You Need to DO

Who Should Do It: ✔ Crisis Coordinator/head administrator of affected school
  ✔ School secretaries/receptionists
  ✔ Campus Liaison
  ✔ Bus drivers
  ✔ Media Liaison
  ✔ Counseling Liaison
  ✔ Teachers
  ✔ Custodial staff
  ✔ Central office staff
  ✔ Parent/Family Liaison
  ✔ All crisis response team members

❏ The highest administrator of the affected school present should organize (or reorganize) your crisis response team—if this was not done in the first hour—and devise a way to identify your crisis response team/authorized volunteers (e.g., with armbands, vests, hats, or ID tags). Strive to select a form of identification that the press can't easily duplicate.

❏ The Crisis Coordinator should appoint a backup in case he or she is occupied for any length of time or becomes ill during the crisis response. An assistant principal is the logical person to fill this role.

❏ The Crisis Coordinator should decide whether to keep the school open for the rest of the day and, if so, what bell schedule to use. If the majority of the staff have it "together" enough to assist your students, it's best for the students (with the exception of very young ones) to remain in school, where they will be assisted in coping with the crisis. But if many staff members are significantly affected by the crisis, cancel school to give them time to deal with their own issues and to formulate a crisis response.

❑ Set and publicize the time for the family/community meeting to be held the evening of the crisis, if this was not done in the first hour. Post this information on the marquee in front of your school and on your school's Web site, and update the telephone "hotline" message for your school. Publicize the time for the meeting on your school system's television station, if there is one. Have your school secretaries/receptionists provide this information to all callers.

❑ Finish the Crisis Fact Sheet, if this was not done in the first hour. The Crisis Fact Sheet should be a *working document*—update it as additional facts are verified throughout the day.

❑ The Campus Liaison should communicate all the facts about the crisis and decisions made—including the schedule for the day—to the faculty, support staff, and the bus drivers who serve your school. Use the Crisis Fact Sheet.

❑ The Campus Liaison should tell all staff members that only the Media Liaison and/or Crisis Coordinator are to provide any information to the media.

❑ Outline ways the faculty and the bus drivers can be of assistance to the students. (*See "Modifying the Curriculum" in Section Six of this booklet and "Childhood/Adolescent Crisis Reactions" in Section Seven of this booklet.*)

❑ The bus drivers serving your school should convey to students that no matter how bad things are, they are safe on the bus. The students should load, ride, and unload the buses in as normal a manner as possible. The bus drivers can communicate concern and control by making eye contact/speaking with students as they load.

❑ The Media Liaison should announce and hold the first press conference as soon as is feasible (*see "Preparing for a Press Conference" and "Holding a Press Conference" in Section Three of this booklet*). Continue to hold press conferences every two to three hours throughout the day, even if there is no new information to announce.

❑ The Media Liaison should communicate with the families of victims and suspected student perpetrator(s) throughout the day to lend support and serve as a go-between with the media (*see "Containing the Media" in Section Three of this booklet*).

❑ The Campus Liaison should help to evaluate your school's need for outside assistance and should assign any volunteers assisting the school their tasks for the day. (*See all related points in Section Four of this booklet, "Help Is at Hand," for guidelines and resources.*)

❑ If you are keeping the school open for the rest of the day, begin to attend to the needs of your students. The students will need the opportunity to process their reactions to the crisis; this effort should be coordinated by the Counseling Liaison. (*See all related points in Section Five of this booklet, "Emotional Recovery in a Crisis," plus "Childhood/ Adolescent Crisis Reactions" in Section Seven of this booklet for complete guidelines.*)

❑ Don't expect the rest of the day to be "business as usual." Modify/set aside the regular curriculum (especially any scheduled tests) at least for the day. Teachers should allow their students to continue to express their feelings through alternate

continued—

activities, such as artwork, writing, listening to appropriate music, and/or drama. (*See "Modifying the Curriculum" in Section Six of this booklet for a brief list of suggested activities pertaining to crises for use by teachers and counselors.*)

❏ The Campus Liaison should continue to communicate updated information to the school's internal audience throughout the day. This information would include the victims' medical conditions, details about any funerals that have been set, status of suspected perpetrator(s), etc.

❏ The Parent/Family Liaison should begin to plan the family/community meeting to be held the evening of the crisis (*see "When/Where to Hold a Family/Community Meeting" and related points later in this section*) early enough in the day to arrange for the attendance of speakers from outside your school.

❏ Create and photocopy a parent/family information packet for use at the meeting. The packet should contain at the least the following information: the most updated version of the Crisis Fact Sheet; information pertinent to the nature of the crisis (e.g., relevant district policies, copies of state laws, etc.); a description of the counseling services available to students/family members through the school and community agencies, with contact information (*see "Providing Counseling Services" in Section Seven of this booklet*); and information about children's typical reactions to trauma/grief and suggestions for assisting children at home (*see "Childhood/Adolescent Crisis Reactions" in Section Seven of this booklet*).

❏ The Parent/Family Liaison, Crisis Coordinator, and any other available team members should collaborate on writing a letter to be sent home to parents. (The Crisis Coordinator should sign off on its content before it is distributed.) The letter should clearly explain what occurred and what you have done to resolve the crisis/its effects, should mention the time of the family/community meeting to be held that evening, and should encourage all parents to attend. It should also specify whether school will be in session the next day. (*See "Task List" in Chapter Two of the main* Coping With Crisis *book for a sample parent letter.*) Include the Crisis Fact Sheet with this letter.

❏ Before the students leave for the day, have all teachers give their classes a quick lesson on media basics. Make sure your students understand that they do not have to talk to reporters just because they are asked a question. (*See "Containing the Media" in Section Three of this booklet.*)

❏ Monitor the dismissal of your students. How you handle the dismissal will be different depending upon the nature/severity of the crisis and whether your school is remaining open or closing early. Take whatever steps are appropriate to safeguard the physical safety and emotional well being of your students.

❏ The Crisis Coordinator, Counseling Liaison, and possibly members of an outside team assisting your school (*see "National Crisis Response Teams/ Organizations" and "State Crisis Response Teams" in Section Four of this booklet*) should visit injured school community members and families of the injured/deceased at the hospital and/or victims' homes. These visits should take place at the earliest possible time during the day or evening of the crisis and should be made in person. Deliver condolences and emphasize the school assistance that will be available to surviving siblings.

❑ When the police have finished working in the area in which the violence/crisis occurred (which may be on the first day or not for several days) and give clearance to alter the area, the custodial staff should clean up the worst of the damage (e.g., wipe up any blood). They should collect victims' personal items that have been strewn about, but should not attempt to erase the victims' presence. Also, school administrators should not immediately eliminate all evidence that the crisis occurred (e.g., patching bullet holes). (*See "Steps to Take After a Crisis" in Section Six of this booklet for points on making such changes.*)

❑ Utilize your prearranged staff calling tree to continue updates of crisis facts outside of school hours. (If you don't already have a calling tree in place, assign a member of your school's support staff to create one before the end of the day.)

❑ The Crisis Coordinator should keep lines of communication open with the police and/or district attorney's office, the Medical Liaison/hospital staff, and families of victims and should communicate any new information to the superintendent, school board, and area schools via the central office.

❑ Eat something—you need fuel to keep yourself going. The crisis response team should stay hydrated by drinking lots of water and should try to squeeze in a break for a few minutes at least every two to three hours. Someone should be put in charge of bringing crisis response team members food and drinks.

❑ The Counseling Liaison and members of any outside crisis response team assisting your school (*see "National Crisis Response Teams/Organizations" and "State Crisis Response Teams" in Section Four of this booklet*) should lead a meeting in which the staff can process their own reactions to the crisis. This meeting can be held either during the school day or right after school and should be *mandatory* for all school staff (with the exception of bus drivers, if the meeting is held after school). (*See all related points in Section Five of this booklet, "Emotional Recovery in a Crisis," plus "Adult Crisis Reactions" in Section Seven of this booklet for complete guidelines.*) Though you may be exhausted and very busy, taking time to work with the staff members may help to ensure that the students will receive the assistance and emotional support they need from their teachers/other staff when they return to school the next day.

❑ Schedule a mandatory faculty meeting for the next morning so that the Campus Liaison can review the plan for the day (including the bell schedule) and ways the faculty can assist their students. Before this meeting the Campus Liaison and/or Counseling Liaison should prepare a handout on tips for teachers to deal with a tragedy at school. (*For suggestions on its content, see "Modifying the Curriculum" in Section Six of this booklet and "Childhood/Adolescent Crisis Reactions" in Section Seven.*)

continued—

❏ At the end of the school day, the Campus Liaison should meet with any volunteer caregivers who assisted the school to collect information from them and thank them for their assistance. (*See "Making the Most of Outside Assistance" in Section Four of this booklet.*)

❏ Keep your school building open into the evening and accessible for staff and students and their family members. Have a counselor from your school/district, crisis response team, or any outside crisis response team assisting your school (*see "National Crisis Response Teams/Organizations" and "State Crisis Response Teams" in Section Four of this booklet*) available to assist members of the school community. (Also have these people available at the school the next day, even if it's a holiday, prescheduled inservice day, or weekend.) Clergy members and/or volunteer mental health practitioners could assist with this support (*see "Local Caregivers/Agencies to Assist in a Crisis" and "Making the Most of Outside Assistance" in Section Four of this booklet*).

❏ Hold the family/community meeting at your school at the appointed time of the evening (*see "Sample Agenda for a Family/Community Meeting" later in this section*).

❏ The Media Liaison should hold the final press conference of the day right after the family/community meeting (*see "Sample Agenda for a Family/ Community Meeting" later in this section*).

❏ The entire crisis response team should meet after the family/community meeting to plan the next day and process team members' reactions to the crisis/crisis response. Discuss each team member's activities during the day; what worked well and what didn't; additional assistance needed by the school/issues concerning outside agencies or individuals; assignments/main tasks of all team members and volunteers for the next day; updated crisis facts and necessary changes to the Crisis Fact Sheet; media/public relations strategies; and emotions experienced by team members during the crisis response.

Responsibilities of School Staff Members

What You Need to KNOW

- Every member of the school community—from support staff to faculty—has a role to play in the crisis response. It is important for all concerned to understand what they are to do (and not do) during and after a severe crisis. This understanding will lessen the anxiety of school staff and help to ensure an effective crisis response.

- The key is for all school community members to follow the instructions of the Crisis Coordinator/head administrator of your school. Additionally, it will be helpful for staff members to assist the members of the crisis response team in whatever ways become necessary throughout the crisis. This is not the time to quibble over the everyday school hierarchy or responsibilities.

- The most important message to convey is that your school community has what it takes to survive the crisis and that you will pull through it by working together. Remain positive about your school's crisis response and resiliency.

- Strive to respect the needs, fears, and concerns of all staff members. Provide permission for a range of emotions, and be careful that the emotional needs of the adults in the school are not overlooked in the focus on assisting students and family members.

What You Need to DO

Who Should Do It: ✔ Crisis Coordinator/head administrator of affected school
✔ All crisis response team members
✔ Support/front office staff (school secretaries/ receptionists, bus drivers, custodial staff)
✔ Teachers
✔ Campus Liaison

❑ *To locate page references for specific actions the Crisis Coordinator should take during the crisis response, see the "Key to the Checklists by Individual" at the end of this booklet.*

❑ *To locate page references for specific actions that each team member should take during the crisis response, see the "Key to the Checklists by Individual" at the end of this booklet.*

❑ *To locate page references for specific actions that various support/front office staff (e.g., secretaries/receptionists, bus drivers, custodial staff) should take during the crisis response, see the "Key to the Checklists by Individual" at the end of this booklet. (NOTE:* The Campus Liaison should reference these pages so that he or she can communicate these responsibilities to appropriate staff members.)

❑ *To locate page references for specific actions that teachers should take during the crisis response, see the "Key to the Checklists by Individual" at the end of this booklet. (NOTE:* The Campus Liaison should reference these pages so that he or she can communicate these responsibilities to appropriate staff members.)

Why to Hold a Family/Community Meeting

What You Need to KNOW

- The goal of the family/community meeting is twofold: (1) to impart information, and (2) to assist the family and community members in processing their reactions to the crisis.

- Schools are often hesitant to hold an open meeting for family and community members, but there is no better way of ensuring that all of their questions are answered, your school's crisis response plans are communicated, and parents learn helpful ways to address the emotional needs of their children.

continued—

- Family/community meetings are an effective way to assist your students, as the speakers help parents understand the typical childhood reactions to a crisis and encourage them to respond with patience, love, tolerance, and support.

- When you give people the time and permission to express their feelings after a crisis, those feelings become validated, leading to a return to normalcy more quickly.

When/Where to Hold a Family/Community Meeting

What You Need to DO

Who Should Do It: ✔ Parent/Family Liaison

❑ Hold a family/community meeting on the evening of the first day of the crisis.

❑ Hold this meeting during the evening hours, when most parents can attend. Six or seven o'clock is best.

❑ Plan for the meeting to take approximately two hours. A meeting much longer than two hours may overwhelm the audience. If it appears that more than two hours or so will be needed, schedule an additional meeting for the following evening.

❑ It is vitally important that this meeting be held at the school, rather than at any location off-campus (e.g., a parent's home).

Who Participates In and Attends a Family/Community Meeting

What You Need to KNOW

- The higher the level of the people leading this meeting, the more concern will be communicated to the audience (e.g., the sheriff is preferred to a lower level police spokesperson).

- If the crisis was catastrophic, consider asking your state's attorney general and/or governor to speak. The superintendent should extend such an invitation, if applicable.

What You Need to DO

Who Should Do It:
- ✔ Security Liaison
- ✔ Central office staff (superintendent or associate superintendent)
- ✔ Crisis Coordinator/head administrator of affected school
- ✔ Medical Liaison
- ✔ All crisis response team members

❑ Invite all your students and their family members, the staff and their family members, and other concerned community members to attend the family/community meeting. (Extend this invitation to telephone callers, through a parent letter, in interviews with the media, etc., as discussed previously.)

❑ Bar the media—even the local media—from attending. Post the Security Liaison at the school's entrance to deny them access and to announce that there will be a press conference right after the meeting.

❑ Facilitating this meeting should be a group effort. Plan to include (as applicable) the superintendent/associate superintendent; the Crisis Coordinator/head administrator of the affected school; a police spokesperson; the district attorney; a victims' advocate; a hospital/medical representative or the Medical Liaison; all crisis response team members; additional counseling staff from your school/district; the members of any outside crisis response team assisting your school (*see "National Crisis Response Teams/Organizations" and "State Crisis Response Teams" in Section Four of this booklet*); and perhaps the Red Cross.

Sample Agenda for a Family/Community Meeting

What You Need to KNOW

- Plan to spend the first half of the meeting providing information, and make the second half an open forum. Let the audience do most of the talking in the second half; they'll need plenty of time to ask questions and vent their emotions.

- Administrators are often uncomfortable delving into the emotionality of a crisis situation. But the more you do so, the more you will help your school and community as a whole. Providing the opportunity to "let off emotional steam" is important: It helps people begin working on a new start. Thus, be sure to include the important second half of the family/community meeting in which processing crisis reactions can take place.

- During a severe crisis, shaken parents and students may not want to be out of one another's sight. It's fine to address the adults and students (even young ones) together.

continued—

What You Need to DO

Who Should Do It: ✔ Crisis Coordinator/head administrator of affected school
✔ Media Liaison
✔ All crisis response team members

two

❑ As people arrive for the meeting, give them the parent/family information packet created earlier in the day (*see "First-Day Task List" previously in this section*), which should include the most updated Crisis Fact Sheet and any other pertinent information (e.g., copies of relevant district policies, state laws, etc.).

❑ *See the sample agenda for a two-hour family/community meeting designed to address the effects of a severe school crisis provided in the "How/Agenda" section of Chapter Two of the main* Coping With Crisis *book. This agenda can serve as a guide to conducting your own family/community meeting.*

❑ The Media Liaison should hold a press conference right after the meeting, outside the school. Gather the media representatives as far away as is feasible from the door from which the audience members will be leaving. Respect the privacy of any audience members who discussed their reactions to the crisis during the meeting: Do not repeat their comments to the media.

❑ Provide the media with a copy of the parent/family information packet used in the family/community meeting.

❑ Review with the media the boundaries that are being enforced for them, and announce the time and location of the first press conference the next day.

section three

section three

Here Come the Media

This section outlines a plan for working with the media that is designed to balance their need to report on the event with your school's need for the time and space to respond to the crisis. This two-pronged approach to working with the media during a school crisis involves "containment" and "cooperation."

Typical Media Response to School Crises

What You Need to KNOW

- A school crisis will almost always draw media attention (either local or national, depending upon the severity of the crisis). Thus, you must have a plan for dealing with the media.

- The media have a job to do and will do it with or without your help. It's in your best interest to cooperate with the media and help them to report a factually accurate story.

- You can't make the media go away, and you can't for the most part control what they say, whom they talk to, what they film/photograph, or who covers the story. However, you can set some limits for appropriate media coverage on your campus.

- If the media have arrived at your school, they're going to leave with a story. What story they tell will depend in large part upon your response.

Containing the Media

What You Need to KNOW

- Containment means setting appropriate limits for the media representatives who are covering your school.

- Containment helps ensure that the media will cover the story without excessive or gratuitous footage of carnage and mourning school community members.

continued—

- Containment does not mean staying silent! It is imperative that you provide the media with the information they need as quickly as possible. (*See the related points in the remainder of this section for guidelines.*)

- If the Media Liaison is also the head administrator of the affected school, have the central office manage all media requests in order to free up this person's time.

three

What You Need to DO

Who Should Do It: ✔ Security Liaison
                      ✔ Media Liaison
                      ✔ Campus Liaison
                      ✔ Teachers
                      ✔ Parent/Family Liaison

❑ Deny the media access to your campus, using your school's security personnel/Security Liaison, the police, and, if absolutely necessary, the National Guard (*see "Securing the Crime Scene and Containing the Media" in Section One of this booklet*).

❑ Direct the media to gather in an off-campus location—such as a room in the central office or a nearby school—for press conferences. (They will probably resist doing so, and you may fare no better than detaining them across the street.)

❑ Do not provide names of victims or suspected student perpetrator(s) until family members have been notified (*see "Injury/Death Notification" in Chapter One of the main* Coping With Crisis *book and "Communicating With Parents/Other Family Members" in Section One of this booklet for more information*).

❑ Do not provide photos of, or personal information about, such people.

❑ Do not provide the names of witnesses to the violence, the names of friends/family members of victims or suspected student perpetrator(s), or the names of students/staff in nearby classrooms.

❑ The Campus Liaison should clearly communicate to all staff members that *only the Media Liaison and/or Crisis Coordinator are to provide any information to any media representative at any time during the crisis.*

❑ Ask the faculty to instruct their students in media basics before the students leave school on the first day of the crisis. The teachers should make sure the students understand that they do not *have* to talk to reporters just because they are asked a question. Teachers should provide the students with a verbal line of defense, such as: "I don't want to talk to you," "Please leave me alone," "Don't take my picture," or, for older students, "No comment."

❑ If necessary, the Security Liaison/police should direct the students to leave the school by side entrances to help shield them from a media barrage.

❏ The Parent/Family Liaison should advise all family members who arrive at the school to not discuss the crisis with reporters as they leave (*see "Communicating With Parents/Other Family Members" in Section One of this booklet*). In particular, the family members should not provide personal information about victims or suspected student perpetrator(s) and their families.

❏ If the families of victims and suspected student perpetrator(s) welcome your assistance, ask if you can "run interference" with the media for them. Throughout the day of the crisis as well as in the days following, you could lend the families support by serving as a go-between with the media. You could, for example, share with the media appropriate information about the victims/suspected student perpetrator(s) and/or the families' statements.

❏ Deny the media access to all family/community meetings held after the crisis. (*See "Who Participates In and Attends a Family/Community Meeting" and "Sample Agenda for a Family/Community Meeting" in Section Two of this booklet*.)

Cooperating With the Media

What You Need to KNOW

- Cooperating with the media means providing them with the information they need to accurately report the story.

- Do not even contemplate refusing to speak with the media. There will be many detrimental effects of such a decision for your school and community.

- Media relations is not part of most school administrators' training. Thus, administrators may fail to take action with the media because they are afraid they will make the situation worse or be blamed for the crisis. In truth, as the school's leader, the administrator will be judged instead for how he or she *responds* to the crisis. Your school must work with the media.

Preparing for a Press Conference

What You Need to KNOW

- Media representatives will want you to talk to them individually; instead, give all the media the same story at one time through press conferences.

- If the Media Liaison is not also the head administrator of the affected school, the media will want to hear from the administrator (and in severe crises, likely the superintendent as well). He or she should use the same procedures as specified in this section for the Media Liaison, who can help to prepare the administrator(s) for the interview(s).

continued—

- The media—including local media—will be barred from attending the family/community meeting to be held the evening of the crisis. To help contain the media, plan to hold a short press conference outside the school after that family/community meeting. (*See "Sample Agenda for a Family/Community Meeting" in Section Two of this booklet for additional information.*)

three

What You Need to DO

Who Should Do It: ✔ Media Liaison
                     ✔ Crisis Coordinator/head administrator of affected school

❏ As soon as is feasible, announce the time/location of the first press conference. Make it clear that your school will be cooperating with the media and that they are to leave your students and staff alone.

❏ Continue to hold press conferences every two to three hours throughout the day, even if there is no new information to announce. When there's no new information, emphasize your school's/district's policies and prevention programs and provide information about the crisis management steps that the school is taking.

❏ Provide a sign-in sheet and ID stickers for media representatives who attend press conferences.

❏ Develop three to five key messages to emphasize during the press conference.

❏ Incorporate these messages into a written statement that you can read to the media at the press conference. Base this press release on the Crisis Fact Sheet and include pertinent district policies/procedures (e.g., those pertaining to weapons and "zero tolerance").

❏ Gear your statements to a broadcast audience. Speak in short, clear, fact-filled sentences, and try to use catch phrases that quickly and clearly communicate your school's message and will be appropriate as "*sound bites.*"

❏ Have more than one person double-check the accuracy of the press release information, and have the Crisis Coordinator/head administrator sign off on its content. Also be sure it contains only medically/legally correct information.

❏ Before the press conference, take the time to rehearse what you are going to say. Have someone fire questions at you to warm you up before you address the media.

❏ In addition to press conferences, you might consider granting reasonable requests for the media to interview administrators, counselors, and crisis response team members. Do not allow interviews of students and staff members.

❏ Before granting interview requests, require that you be given prior knowledge of the interview's subject matter. You might also require that your school district's attorney be present during all interviews.

Holding a Press Conference

What You Need to KNOW

- *If the tragedy is a suicide of a school community member, see "Media Coverage of Suicides" in Section Eleven of this booklet for important information.* The media coverage of a suicide must be handled with extreme delicacy in order to safeguard the other students.

What You Need to DO

Who Should Do It: ✔ Media Liaison
✔ Crisis Coordinator/head administrator of affected school
✔ Central office staff (superintendent or designee)

Making Your Statement

☐ Begin the press conference by asking the media to hold all questions until after you've made your statements.

☐ Always release information regarding student/staff safety first.

☐ Do not release the names of victims/suspected student perpetrator(s) before their families have been notified, and do not provide personal information about such individuals.

☐ Give all the known facts of the crisis in a complete and truthful manner. Do not attempt to cover up any aspect of the incident. The reporters will uncover the whole story, and you will lose credibility.

☐ Tell the media what the school is doing to fix the problem: Explain the crisis plan and emphasize that the school is doing everything possible to respond in an appropriate manner and that the school and district care about the situation.

☐ Emphasize any preparatory actions being taken by your school and district and the emotional support being provided to staff and students.

☐ Utilize the media to dispense important information about assistance available to the community. State the time/location of the family/community meeting to be held the evening of the crisis and say that the school encourages all family members and affected community members to attend. Highlight actions parents can take to help their children cope with the effects of the crisis. Also emphasize that the school will be in session the next day and that it will be beneficial for all students to be in attendance.

☐ Detail the school's plan for the following day, emphasizing the emotional support to be delivered to students by trained staff members.

continued—

❑ After providing all the pertinent facts, take a few minutes to focus on prevention and any prevention programs your district has in place.

❑ If applicable, emphasize that violence is a societal problem—not just a school problem—and that violence prevention involves a *community-wide* (indeed, a society-wide) effort.

Answering Media Questions

❑ When taking questions from the media, repeat the question before giving your answer. Don't forget to breathe.

❑ If you are asked a question that really "throws you," ask the reporter to repeat the question. This buys you a little time to compose an appropriate answer.

❑ Set the pace of the press conference. Take the time you need before answering questions to think clearly about your answers. Do not blurt out the first thing that comes into your mind because you are feeling pressured.

❑ Answer only one question at a time, and ignore interruptions. Remain calm and communicate clearly.

❑ Ignore inappropriate questions, if possible. Or say, "That's not what we need to focus on at this time," or "I'm sorry, I can't provide that information."

❑ You can also rephrase inappropriate questions posed by the media and then answer the rephrased questions by providing your key points.

❑ Answer *all* questions related to student/staff safety.

❑ Limit your comments to school issues. Don't comment on questions that should be answered by the police, and ask the police spokesperson to not make statements on behalf of your school.

❑ Do not speculate. Discuss only the *facts* of the crisis. If you are asked about something you do not know, say that you don't know. Or say, "That information has not been confirmed. We will update you when we know for certain."

❑ Be yourself. Talk in your normal tone of voice using your everyday vocabulary.

❑ Be sincere, and express your sadness and dismay about what has happened. However, avoid saying, "I am sorry," which implies guilt and invites blame of the school/district.

❑ Ask the media to refrain from glamorizing the suspected perpetrator(s) with excessive attention. Remind them that children are attention seekers and that a focus on the perpetrator(s) could contribute to future "copycat" incidents. Ask the media to instead focus on the needs of survivors.

❑ Remind the media that there are approximately 37 million public school children in the country who could potentially be exposed to their coverage. Encourage them to use restraint in publicizing details that could terrify young viewers.

❏ Remind the media that you will provide them with all pertinent information as it becomes available and direct them to leave your students, staff, and their families alone. Announce the time of the next scheduled press conference.

❏ At the end of the press conference, provide the media representatives with copies of the Crisis Fact Sheet and any preexisting fact sheet about your campus/district.

After the Press Conference

What You Need to DO

Who Should Do It: ✔ Media Liaison

❏ Throughout the day, attempt to build rapport with the media representatives to reinforce the importance of privacy/confidentiality for all parties (e.g., victims and their family members).

❏ To nip media speculation in the bud, visit the editorial board of your local newspaper(s) within 24-48 hours to give your side of the story.

❏ Monitor television/radio coverage of your school's crisis throughout the day and evening. Ask that a correction be broadcast if any inaccurate information is reported.

Media Plan for After the Crisis

What You Need to KNOW

- Expect that the media will likely be back at your school on the days following the crisis as well as on "milestone" dates: the end of the school year, graduation day, the beginning of the next school year, and anniversaries of the crisis.

What You Need to DO

Who Should Do It: ✔ Media Liaison
                              ✔ Security Liaison

❏ The Media Liaison and Security Liaison should arrive at the school early on the day after the crisis (as well as on the days following). Arriving by no later than 7:30 AM should ensure that you arrive there before the media, enabling you to contain the media and most likely make the morning (and possibly noon hour) news.

❏ If there is no new information to announce, review the school's concern for safety, its record of school safety (if it is a good one), and the steps being taken to secure the campus and assist the students. Also discuss the positive effects of the family/community meeting held the prior evening.

continued—

❏ Media coverage may last from one day to a week or more, and in smaller communities the local media may follow up for a long time after the crisis. The media may also approach you on "milestone" dates of the crisis. Shift the focus of the later interviews from the suspected perpetrator(s) to prevention efforts and the need for healing/resolution within your school and community.

❏ Long after the crisis, every time there is a similar incident in your district, city, state, or even elsewhere in the country, the media may approach you. To aid in the long-term recovery of your school, consider denying interview requests. If you do speak with the media, limit your comments to a positive, generic statement about education and your school's own prevention programs.

section four

Help Is at Hand

This section covers recommended actions for dealing with the help that will likely be offered to your school during a severe crisis. Some of the individuals and organizations that offer assistance will be truly helpful to you, others will probably not be. The following checklists provide tips on determining whose help to accept and outline human and financial resources available at the local, state, and national level. Suggestions for effectively using those volunteers you do authorize to help your school are also given, so that you can reap the maximum benefit from their assistance. Finally, a few tips on avoiding the pitfalls of the "politics" of crisis response are also provided.

Cautions in Accepting Outside Assistance

What You Need to KNOW

- The help that arrives at your school soon after a crisis is publicized may or may not be the help you need. You need a plan for when, when not, and how to utilize these people.

- Well meaning but misguided helpers can do more harm than good, and some may have their own agenda (e.g., building up their private practice, gaining publicity, or selling services to your district). Beware the charlatans who try to profit from your tragedy.

- The best people to assist with a school crisis are other school people. In a large school system, you may have all the help you need (with the exception of a specially trained state/national crisis response team) within your own district. Both large and small school systems should accept the help of anyone from within their district.

- As a general rule, you can safely accept the assistance of any county or regional mental health association without checking references.

- Do not use private therapists unless you already have an established relationship with these people (i.e., a relationship developed before the crisis) and they are familiar with your school. Psychiatrists also are not usually the answer during a crisis—most have no hands-on experience working in schools.

continued—

- Mental health practitioners specializing in grief counseling, child development/ therapy, trauma, or post-traumatic stress disorder would be most helpful during a school crisis.

- Members of the clergy can provide a calming presence and a shoulder to cry on, particularly in communities with fewer mental health resources available or those with strong ties to local churches. However, these helpers should refrain from imposing their religious beliefs upon your school community unless the staff/students/family members are members of their congregations.

four

What You Need to DO

Who Should Do It: ✔ Campus Liaison (and possibly the Counseling Liaison)
                            ✔ Security Liaison

❏ If you decide to allow private mental health practitioners to help in your school, it is important to screen each volunteer to determine if his or her presence would be beneficial. The Campus Liaison (and the Counseling Liaison, if necessary) should ask each of these people: "How well do you know adolescents (or the age group of your students)?" "What does your practice specialize in?" "Have you helped any other schools when there has been a crisis?" And if so, "Whom did you help?" Then take the time to call the school(s) where the practitioner has assisted in the past. Insist upon a recommendation or referral.

❏ If anyone volunteering his or her assistance refuses to leave when politely told "no thank-you," call for the Security Liaison.

❏ Pair each clergy member with a counseling staff member from within your school system. (*See "Role of the Clergy" in Chapter Nine of the main* Coping With Crisis *book for additional guidelines and information to provide to clergy members assisting your school.*)

Help to Request During a School Crisis

What You Need to KNOW

- While caution in evaluating outside assistance is wise, it is not advisable to close your doors to everyone. Consider the scope of the crisis and carefully evaluate whether you may need some additional help.

- Schools may hesitate to ask for help during a crisis because they believe their crisis isn't important/severe enough to warrant the assistance of others, but people's emotions are always important regardless of whether one person was hurt or ten. Don't underestimate the effects of a crisis on your school and community.

- Do not resist outside assistance because you fear you will lose control of your school. This won't happen unless you have absolutely no action plan in place. (By following the recommended actions in this booklet, that is guaranteed not to be the case.) You will need the support of your central office. In addition, you will likely need help from police/emergency responders and possibly many others.

- The more severe the crisis, the more assistance will be required. It's almost impossible to have too much help during a crisis, and an over-response is always preferable to an under-response.

- Asking for outside assistance doesn't mean that your crisis response team "can't handle it." It means that you are capable and caring enough to do whatever it takes to help your school/community. Help yourselves by allowing others to help you in your time of need.

four

Local Caregivers/Agencies to Assist in a Crisis

What You Need to KNOW

- The most obvious resources in any school crisis are other school people. Any school psychologists/counselors from within the district willing to help your school should be released by their supervisors to go to the scene immediately. Even scheduled special education meetings should take a backseat to a timely and comprehensive crisis response.

- Members of student assistance teams, student/staff support teams (SSTs), and teacher assistance teams (TATs) in your school/neighboring schools can help with counseling. Such teams, or your PTA/PTO, could also assist your crisis response team by answering phones, making copies, etc.

- Particularly when a crisis is severe, you might benefit from speaking to staff members of another school (in your town, state, or another state) who have gone through a similar ordeal. They will be able to offer practical advice and emotional support.

- Each county/municipality has an emergency management agency. While generally called on after natural disasters, this agency also can be helpful to your school after an act of violence. The agency staff members are familiar with medical facilities, crowd control, and coordination with law enforcement/other agencies.

- Coordinating the crisis response with appropriate city officials will benefit not only your school but your community as a whole.

- If your school/district is unprepared/understaffed to manage the media onslaught, you might hire a reputable local public relations firm with experience in schools or consult with the National School Public Relations Association (NSPRA) in Rockville, Maryland: (301) 519-0496 or www.gspra.org/nspra.html

continued—

- Your local telephone service company might provide you with additional equipment (e.g., pagers, telephone lines, and cellular phones) on a temporary basis. Before using cellular phones, check to ensure that they cause no interference for police/other emergency responders' communication systems. Also be aware that cellular phone calls are not secure. Whatever is discussed can be monitored and used inappropriately by the media.

What You Need to DO

four

Who Should Do It: ✔ Campus Liaison
✔ Crisis Coordinator/head administrator of affected school

❏ Access any school resources (from area schools, within your district or school system) available to you first.

❏ Ask administrators within your district to temporarily release from their everyday responsibilities any school psychologists and/or counselors willing to help your school.

❏ Contact your local mental health association (e.g., for the county) to begin accessing regional/state mental health workers. The victims' advocate in the prosecutor's office of your local courts will also be able to assist you in locating appropriate mental health assistance.

❏ If your local university/college has a psychology program, contact the dean or a department head to enlist faculty to assist you.

❏ Communicate with, and involve as appropriate, your city's leaders.

❏ Access any other appropriate local caregivers/agencies.

Judicial/Governmental Assistance

What You Need to KNOW

- The Red Cross can provide food, drinks, and other basic survival supplies (if needed) during the crisis response. Look under "American Red Cross" in the business white pages of your telephone book for the number of your local chapter.

- Every county should have at least one victims' advocate. He or she will help coordinate available services (funded by the state) for victims' families and help them to navigate the legal process. Victims' advocates will usually contact victims and their families; however, you may contact a victims' advocate directly by calling the prosecutor's office of your local courts.

- If absolutely necessary, the National Guard is available to assist with security (e.g., barring the media/other unauthorized persons from accessing your campus, providing specialized military equipment). The governor of your state summons the National Guard, and your superintendent should request this assistance, if needed, from that office.

- Regardless of whether the National Guard assists your school after a crisis, the state police can provide a great deal of support at the site. They will help provide a sense of security for survivors, as well as assist with containing the media and with transportation/police escort needs.

- State government leaders such as the governor and attorney general can offer valuable assistance. Careful planning can minimize media attention and potential political implications.

What You Need to DO

Who Should Do It: ✔ Campus Liaison
✔ Crisis Coordinator/head administrator of affected school
✔ Central office staff (superintendent)

☐ Contact the appropriate judicial/governmental departments or agencies to request human resource assistance. Involve the Crisis Coordinator and, if appropriate, the superintendent in such requests.

National Crisis Response Teams/Organizations

What You Need to KNOW

National Organization for Victim Assistance (NOVA)

- Founded in 1975 in Washington, D.C., the National Organization for Victim Assistance (NOVA) is a private, nonprofit organization working on behalf of victims of crime and other crises (e.g., natural disasters).

- NOVA provides direct services to victims by sending Community Crisis Response Teams (CCRTs) to respond to crises around the nation and the world.

- In a severe crisis, the leaders/caregivers of your school and community may be in distress themselves. And, they may be unsure about what to do to help, since *few people (including school psychologists/counselors) are trained specifically in using their helping skills in catastrophic situations.* For these reasons, a national team can be very helpful.

- A NOVA team will come to your community for no more than three to four days to offer information/suggestions on how to respond to your community's distress. Trained team members will help your local decision makers identify those most affected by the crisis; provide support/training to your local caregivers; and lead one or more community-wide forums to help your community members begin to cope with their distress.

continued—

- All NOVA team members are volunteers, with only their travel/lodging expenses covered by the local community or by donations to NOVA. NOVA teams are sent only where they are invited. NOVA will quickly send a crisis response team to any community in crisis that requests NOVA's assistance.

National Emergency Assistance Team (NEAT)

- The National Association of School Psychologists (NASP) formed the National Emergency Assistance Team (NEAT) in 1996 to facilitate the psychological well being of students/school staff and enable schools to quickly resume their regular activities following a large-scale emergency.

- Currently, NASP has funding to dispatch the NEAT team to only one national crisis per year. (Additional funds can be requested/approved by the NASP Executive Board quickly after a severe crisis.)

- A NOVA/NEAT professional alliance has been formed to better serve schools/children after a crisis. The NEAT team may be able to provide direct, on-site assistance in the aftermath of a major crisis, probably in partnership with NOVA. To request such on-site assistance, make two calls—to NOVA and to NASP. The two organizations will then work together to provide a comprehensive response for your school.

- Even if the NEAT team is not dispatched, NEAT will provide information/resources/handouts pertaining to crisis intervention if contacted by a school district.

- NEAT team members are also available for *telephone consultations* on school crisis response. You may request this help by calling your region's NASP representative during business hours.

Community Crisis Response (CCR)

- A division of the U.S. Department of Justice, the Office for Victims of Crime (OVC) established a Community Crisis Response (CCR) program to improve services for multiple victims of violent crime. The CCR funds individuals/teams to provide debriefings and training to community members and victim service agencies.

What You Need to DO

Who Should Do It: ✔ Campus Liaison
✔ Crisis Coordinator/head administrator of affected school

❑ Discuss whether assistance (either on-site or off) from a national crisis response team and/or school organization might be helpful to you in responding to your severe crisis. Then contact one or more of the following resources for additional information.

❑ Contact NOVA by calling (202) 232-6682 (232-NOVA). This number is staffed 24 hours per day to assist those requesting assistance/information. (*See "Organizations/Agencies" in the Appendix of the main* Coping With Crisis *book for additional NOVA contact information.*)

four

❏ To request that a NEAT team be dispatched (often in partnership with NOVA), contact the National Association of School Psychologists (NASP) office in Bethesda, Maryland, at (301) 657-0270.

❏ For a telephone consultation with a NEAT member, or to request print resources, contact your state's representative. (*See "Organizations/Agencies" in the Appendix of the* main Coping With Crisis *book for a complete list of NEAT contacts by state.*)

❏ Requests for CCR assistance must come from an agency that regularly assists victims of crime, on behalf of your school. Contact Timothy J. Johnson, Community Crisis Response, Office for Victims of Crime, U.S. Department of Justice, 633 Indiana Avenue, NW, Room 1352, Washington, D.C. 20531; (202) 305-4548; (202) 514-6383 (FAX).

❏ For a list of national school organizations (with contact information) that might be appropriate sources of advice/support after a severe school crisis, *see "Organizations/Agencies" in the Appendix of the main* Coping With Crisis *book.*

four

State Crisis Response Teams

What You Need to KNOW

- Currently, Arkansas, Florida, and Kentucky are the only states that we're aware of with a state-level crisis response team.

- Other states may also have state-level crisis response resources available, however, and you are encouraged to investigate this possibility if your school is not in one of the states listed.

What You Need to DO

Who Should Do It: ✔ Campus Liaison
✔ Crisis Coordinator/head administrator of affected school

❏ Discuss whether assistance (either on-site or off) from a state-level crisis response team might be helpful to you in responding to your severe crisis. Then contact your state's team, if it is known to you, or investigate whether any such resources are available in your state.

❏ If you are an Arkansas school experiencing a crisis, contact the Arkansas Crisis Response Team through the Office of the Attorney General, Outreach Division, at (800) 448-3014. (For additional information, contact the office of the Arkansas Deputy Attorney General at [501] 682-6073.)

❏ If you are a Florida school experiencing a crisis, contact Frank Zenere, chair of the Florida Emergency Assistance Team (FEAT), at (305) 995-7319.

continued—

❏ If you are a Kentucky school experiencing a crisis, contact your state's crisis response team at (502) 564-0131 or (888) 522-7228.

❏ To determine whether your state, region, or county has any sort of crisis response team to assist you, you might contact: (1) your state's school psychology association or the National Association of School Psychologists (NASP), in Bethesda, Maryland, at (301) 657-0270; (2) your state's department of education; (3) your county's victims' advocate through your local prosecutor's office; and/or (4) your state's attorney general's office.

four

Making the Most of Outside Assistance

What You Need to KNOW

• Even if an outside crisis response team comes to assist your school, it's important for your school's own team members/staff to remain involved and to actively participate in each step of the crisis response.

• School counselors/psychologists are often not trained in responding to severe crises and may be affected themselves by the incident. For these and other reasons, schools often want an outside team to simply take over, but this isn't best for the school/ community. The outside team members will lend their expertise, but they need you to hang in there and participate in the intervention.

• Only you know the staff, students, and community members, and these people will be counting on you for continued support after any outside experts leave.

• The main role of every authorized volunteer who assists your school (e.g., clergy members) is to simply be an empathetic listener and a caring presence.

What You Need to DO

Who Should Do It: ✔ Campus Liaison (and/or Counseling Liaison)
  ✔ Crisis Coordinator/head administrator of affected school
  ✔ Central office staff

❏ The Campus Liaison should provide all volunteers with paper and pens and ask them to record the names of every school community member with whom they work. For follow-up purposes, have them note those individuals they are particularly worried about. Also review with them the following guidelines:

▪ Volunteers should not tell their religious views or personal stories to whomever they're working with, and should try not to emote.

▪ There are no magic words to say that will set things right. *Wrong* things for volunteers to say include: "I understand," "I know how you feel," and "I felt the same way when . . . ." Instead, they should say, for example, "I can't imagine how difficult this must be."

- Volunteers should provide permission for a range of emotions (even nervous laughter or seeming indifference). Everyone deals with trauma/loss differently, and there is no one correct way to feel at any given time.
- Volunteers should stress the commonality of feelings, emphasizing that whatever someone may be feeling, others feel the same way and it is a normal reaction to the crisis.
- Volunteers should assist the people they are working with in identifying the challenges they will face in the immediate future and their sources of strength/coping skills. Volunteers should try to instill a sense of hope.

❏ At the end of the day, don't let your helpers simply pack up and drive away. The Campus Liaison (and/or Counseling Liaison) should hold a brief meeting with all the volunteer caregivers present to: (1) systematically gather information that will help your school community in the future; (2) formally thank these people for their assistance; and (3) provide the opportunity for the volunteers to "vent."

❏ The Crisis Coordinator/head administrator and a central office representative should attend this meeting so they also can hear the identified needs for the following days.

❏ If any of the volunteers will be coming back the next day to assist again, the Campus Liaison should take the time at the meeting to plan their actions/assignments.

Financial Support Available in a Crisis

What You Need to KNOW

Donated Funds

- In the event of a severe crisis, your school will receive financial assistance from many people and places.
- Most likely, members of your community will begin to collect emergency funds of their own volition.
- If your school's crisis is nationally publicized, you may be surprised at the generosity/ sympathy directed to you from around the country and even the world.
- Your local bank(s)/savings and loan officer can help your school's administrators to establish accounts, trusts, and scholarship funds to manage such donations, as might your local United Way organization.
- The issue of utilizing donated funds is sensitive and requires careful planning. Your school might wish to consult with another school in your state/nationally that has experienced a severe crisis for additional advice on this issue.
- The needs of victims and their families must come first. Spending remaining donations on a lasting memorial that the community can use indefinitely will probably satisfy the largest number of people.

continued—

Requesting Funds

- Your school may be eligible for governmental assistance if you request it. At the state level, the Board of Education might help fund the ongoing crisis response or funds might be allocated from your state's disaster fund, if appropriate. The Department of Education (the Safe and Drug Free Schools monies) and the Federal Emergency Management Agency (FEMA) are two possible sources of federal assistance for funding long-term counseling services and other school/community needs.

- The U.S. Department of Justice's Office for Victims of Crime administers the Crime Victims Fund to support services for crime victims and their families at the state level. Such funds are distributed through each state's Crime Victims Compensation Board. The board is usually administered by the attorney general's office, but in some states it is housed in the governor's office or state department of health. For assistance, contact these agencies for your state or contact the Office for Victims of Crime directly at (202) 307-5983.

- If federal financial assistance is needed, your school should request it as quickly as possible due to the common delays involved in processing/approving such requests.

- Your state's department of education, your governor, your state's attorney general's office, local and state legislators, and congressional representatives could all be helpful in facilitating requests for financial assistance.

- Funds from state and federal sources are generally used to provide direct services to the school (e.g., funding counselors to provide mental health assistance to students and staff) rather than for any sort of memorializing activities.

What You Need to DO

Who Should Do It: ✔ Campus Liaison
✔ Crisis Coordinator/head administrator of affected school
✔ Central office staff (superintendent and/or school board members)

❑ Contact your local bank and/or United Way organization to establish a securely managed account as soon as it is apparent that donations will be coming into your school. Then publicize this account information for the convenience of others wishing to donate.

❑ Establish a representative committee of school personnel (including teachers) and parents to monitor the account(s) and decide together how to spend the donated monies. All other school personnel, students, and perhaps parents should be surveyed for their ideas as well.

❑ *See "Cautions Regarding Memorializing," "Raising and Dispersing Funds," and all related points in Section Six of this booklet for suggestions on utilizing donated funds.*

❏ Your school superintendent/school board should contact appropriate federal, state, city, and county representatives (including your county/municipality's emergency management agency) for advice about and support in requesting financial assistance.

Politics of Crisis Response

What You Need to KNOW

- The more crisis planning that has been done in advance in your school/district, the less chaos and the fewer competing factions there will be surrounding what should be done and who can do it when a crisis occurs.

- During a crisis it is difficult to think clearly, even for those in charge. Thus, conflicts/misunderstandings often arise. It helps to be more patient than usual and to be very clear in your communications/intentions.

- The principle guiding the crisis response should be: "What do those affected by the crisis need and who in the school/community has previously demonstrated competency in meeting such needs?"

- The crisis will exacerbate any communication problems or tensions between competing factions in your school/community, but it also has the potential to help improve such situations.

- During almost every crisis response, there will be problems and concerns, but early discussion and continued collaboration among school/community leaders will help to reduce them.

What You Need to DO

Who Should Do It: ✔ Crisis Coordinator/head administrator of affected school
✔ Central office staff (superintendent and others)
✔ All crisis response team members

❏ Key school, community, and agency leaders should meet early in the crisis response to discuss the specifics of the situation and how best to work collaboratively to address the crisis.

❏ Take the high ground: Do whatever must be done to help the victims/survivors get through the crisis, regardless of your own motivations and political concerns. If everyone involved is truly working toward that goal, the politics of crisis response will be much less disruptive.

❏ It is important for district/school administrators to keep school personnel who provided assistance in the immediate aftermath of the crisis involved in the decision making in the weeks and months ahead.

four

section five

Emotional Recovery in a Crisis

This section outlines a proven model for helping all individuals affected by a crisis to examine their crisis reactions in order to minimize trauma and begin emotional recovery. Such "processing" could be considered "emotional first aid" and is a vital component of the long-term healing of students, staff members (from administrators to support staff), parents/other family members, and even the caregivers in a crisis. The practical suggestions provided here have been tested in various types of real-life crisis situations and have been used successfully by the National Organization for Victim Assistance (NOVA) for two decades. School mental health staff familiar with other "processing" models will find the NOVA model complementary to those other theories and will find it to be a powerful tool for addressing extreme emotionality in the event of a severe school crisis.

Emotional "Processing" Defined/The Need for Processing

What You Need to KNOW

- Processing is simply a way of talking that facilitates discussion about a crisis by those affected by it.
- Reaching out immediately to victims and their families following a crisis can help to prevent the development of post-traumatic symptoms.
- Although children are resilient, they will need the opportunity to process the crisis (and your assistance in doing so).
- Children who verbalize the most and those who attend school most often after a crisis recover the best.
- When you give people the time and permission to express their feelings after a crisis, those feelings become validated, leading to a faster return to normalcy.

continued—

- If your school community members are not provided with opportunities to process their reactions to the crisis at school, they may instead tell their "crisis stories" to the media. Doing so is not necessarily beneficial to the school community members' mental health; they need the assistance of trained school and crisis response personnel after a severe crisis.

- It will be helpful for mental health personnel to be highly visible in your school following a crisis and to proactively seek out those who need their help.

- Be careful not to focus on the needs of your students to the exclusion of affected adults. Your school's staff, for example, must have the opportunity to process the crisis if they are to assist the students.

- Others who would benefit from the opportunity to process their reactions to the crisis include first responders on the scene; witnesses; friends/family members of victims, of suspected student perpetrator(s), and of your students and staff; local caregivers; your crisis response team; and the local media.

Potential Barriers to Processing

What You Need to KNOW

- School leaders may want to focus solely on logistics, ignoring the emotionality of the crisis. Even though this may be more comfortable for them, it will not facilitate healing.

- In addition to students, affected adults in your school and community will need to process their reactions to the crisis. However, in some communities, receiving counseling carries a stigma. It may be necessary to help community members to recognize the difference between short-term counseling for otherwise healthy people after a traumatic event and long-term therapy used to treat any number of mental conditions/disorders. It may also be helpful to explain that short-term assistance is appropriate for *anyone* affected by a crisis, regardless of age, gender, or professional position.

- You may be uncomfortable talking about "feelings." If so, focus instead on "reactions to the crisis." Everyone involved in the crisis at your school has had a reaction to it.

- Some school leaders and community members may believe that processing is unnecessary if your school's crisis was less severe than other highly publicized/catastrophic events (e.g., school shooting incidents) that have happened in our nation's schools in recent years. They must understand, however, that every crisis is important to the individuals who were involved in the incident and that processing is very helpful.

- Some people may think that crises caused by situations other than violence do not necessitate processing. They are wrong. Crises such as a drowning or car accident, for example, would also warrant processing.

- Some people may think processing at school is unnecessary for a crisis incident that occurred off school grounds. However, these incidents often affect the school community and should be processed at school.

- If you do not know *how* to facilitate the processing of crisis effects, your effort to do so may not be very helpful to the participants. *See the remaining points in this section of the booklet for helpful suggestions to ensure effective processing.*

General Processing Guidelines

What You Need to KNOW

five

- We encourage you to utilize principles of the powerful counseling model that has been used by the National Organization for Victim Assistance (NOVA) for two decades and has proven helpful for people of all ages after crises. This model works extremely well one-to-one, with small to mid-size groups (e.g., 50 people), and even with several hundred participants at once. (*NOTE*: For assistance with the model, or to inquire about training for the future, call [202] 232-6682 [232-NOVA]. This number is staffed by NOVA 24 hours per day to assist those requesting assistance/information. *See "Organizations/Agencies" in the Appendix of the main* Coping With Crisis *book for additional contact information for NOVA*.)

- The Crisis Coordinator/head administrator should convey the importance of processing to the staff by participating in the staff session(s). A strong leader can model/openly express emotions and still be respected and admired.

- Hold separate processing sessions for the students and staff. However, adults and children can process together during family/community meetings (*see "Who Participates In and Attends a Family/Community Meeting" and "Sample Agenda for a Family/Community Meeting" in Section Two of this booklet*).

- Give permission for a range of emotions, particularly in the student discussions. Many students won't cry, and some may even laugh nervously when they hear the bad news. Others may say, "I don't care" and cry later. Remember that there is no one correct way to feel at any given time.

- During a processing session, everyone's story is valid. Someone else's story is every bit as important as yours regardless of whether you were standing next to the victim, you almost got hurt, or that other person was at an end of the building far from where the crisis occurred. It's important to provide a forum in which everyone's experiences are listened to and valued.

- Not all participants need to speak during a processing session. Those who do not choose to discuss their crisis reactions will still benefit from hearing others' feelings and recognizing the commonality of their own feelings and those of others.

- The participants may wish to pray during and/or after a processing session. If so, allow time for this. (Prayer is not a required aspect of the model, however.)   *continued—*

What You Need to DO

Who Should Do It: ✔ Counseling Liaison (and possibly other members
of the counseling and/or administrative staffs)
✔ Teachers
✔ Crisis Coordinator/head administrator of affected school

❑ Enlist the involvement of any outside crisis response team assisting your school (*see Section Four of this booklet*) for processing sessions. However, be sure the processing sessions also involve caregivers from within your school/district.

❑ Hold student processing discussions within each affected classroom as soon after the crisis incident as is feasible. (*NOTE*: Very young students, however, should be reunited with their primary caretakers as soon as possible after a traumatic event.) Student processing should occur with groups no larger than classroom size. Ideally, student processing will take place with the assistance of the teacher and at least one counseling staff member (three, if you plan to follow the full NOVA model) or administrator in each affected class.

❑ The Counseling Liaison should lead the staff in processing the crisis either during the day of the crisis if school has been canceled or right after school if the school remains open for the rest of the day. The entire staff (including faculty and support staff) can meet together. The Crisis Coordinator/head administrator should *make this staff processing session mandatory for all* (with the exception of bus drivers if the meeting is held after school).

❑ Process the crisis as close as possible to the crisis scene (i.e., ideally, at the school).

❑ Choose a location that is conducive to discussion and ensures the privacy of those participating.

❑ Bar the media (even the local media) from attending any processing sessions (*see "Who Participates In and Attends a Family/Community Meeting" and "Sample Agenda for a Family/Community Meeting" in Section Two of this booklet for additional guidelines*).

❑ Have drinking water, tissues, and perhaps snacks available.

❑ Allot enough time for the session. If you must limit the time of the processing session, indicate the time limits before the discussion begins.

❑ During the session, note those who may need more in-depth assistance to recover from the crisis (*see "Providing Counseling Services" in Section Seven of this booklet for more information*). Those needing additional assistance may be the obvious people (e.g., close friends/family members of victims or suspected student perpetrator[s], injured survivors, and witnesses). Or they may be people who had no direct involvement in the crisis but who are experiencing a great deal of trauma due to their own history of crisis/loss (unresolved issues may resurface) or due to a lack of coping skills.

❑ Read through/become familiar with all the steps of the NOVA model (*see "The NOVA Processing Model" following*) before implementing it with a group. Alternately, review the procedures of the counseling model in which your school staff has been trained and perhaps identify ways in which principles of the proven NOVA model can be incorporated to complement your model.

The NOVA Processing Model

What You Need to KNOW

- The NOVA model provides a consistent method for processing and instills confidence in your school's caregivers for facilitating processing sessions.

- The model provides participants with the opportunity to process the crisis themselves, which is more therapeutic than just hearing about the need to process!

- The model complements traditional school approaches but places more emphasis on the crisis survivors talking than on the counselors talking.

- All members of the school community—even young children—can understand this approach and participate due to its emphasis on sensory perceptions (i.e., what is seen, heard, tasted, smelled, and felt).

- The NOVA model helps participants to explore their memories of and feelings about an event because it begins with a recall of sensory perceptions.

- The model helps those who have been traumatized to anticipate and plan for their immediate future because it includes a unique "problem-solving" component.

- To implement the full NOVA model you'll need three mental health caregivers per session (e.g., the Counseling Liaison and others); several large sheets of paper and an easel (or tape to attach the papers to a wall); markers (three different colors are preferable); and a chair for each participant (including the Facilitator). The chairs should, when possible, be arranged in a circle or horseshoe.

- You may need to remain flexible about the circle arrangement. With hundreds of people in a session, for example, you won't have room for that many chairs in a circle. Even if you did have the room, the people wouldn't be able to hear one another speaking.

What You Need to DO

Who Should Do It: ✔ Counseling Liaison (and other members of the school's/district's counseling staff and/or outside crisis response team assisting your school)

❑ Gather the needed supplies and arrange the room for the session (e.g., remove all desks and arrange the necessary number of chairs in a circle). The circle of chairs should be as small as possible, with no extra chairs. All participants should be able to hear and see one another.

continued—

five

❑ For each processing session, assign a "Facilitator," a "Scribe," and "Caregiver(s)." The roles of these session leaders are as follows:

Facilitator

- Know the factual details of the trauma.
- Explain the roles of the Scribe and Caregiver(s).
- Clarify the ground rules and emotional security issues, and give permission to the group to say whatever they like.
- Lead the processing session. Maintain emotional control of yourself. (If you start to cry or otherwise emote, the Scribe will need to take over the role of Facilitator for the remainder of the session. If you feel capable, you could become the Scribe for the remainder of the session.)
- Focus completely on the one person who is speaking. Maintain eye contact and an open, accepting body posture. Do not turn your attention from the speaker to any other member of the group, even if someone else is sobbing. (*NOTE*: The exception is if someone interrupts the speaker. You must ask that person to be quiet.)

Scribe

- Provide emotional and practical support to the Facilitator.
- Record the participants' comments on the large pieces of paper so that everyone can see them—
  - Record at least one comment per participant, denoting changes in speaker with a mark/symbol.
  - Write down words and phrases rather than complete sentences, but do not paraphrase.
  - Underline key words/phrases, or use different colors of marker to denote sensory perceptions, problems/challenges, and coping skills.
  - Record selectively. (You won't be able to record everything and keep up.)
  - Stand to the side of the paper so the participants can see what you've written.
- Speak only when called upon by the Facilitator or if the Facilitator becomes emotionally overwhelmed.

Caregiver(s)

- Circulate throughout the room (outside the circle) and quietly assist participants who become distraught.
- Follow any participants who leave the circle and offer them assistance. (If possible, begin and end the session with everyone together.) However, do not ask participants to leave the circle if they have not chosen to do so on their own. Crying is a natural part of the process and should not be treated as a disruption.
- Address the group as a whole only if the Facilitator asks you to do so.

❑ *For step-by-step directions—including scripted statements—for facilitating a processing session, see "The NOVA Model" section of Chapter Five of the main* Coping With Crisis *book.*

section six

The Crisis Aftermath

This section details important actions to take in the days following a crisis incident, including suggestions for temporarily modifying and/or setting aside the regular curriculum to facilitate the emotional recovery of students. Additionally, funeral procedures are outlined, as are guidelines for memorializing activities by students, the school, and community members.

Steps to Take After a Crisis

What You Need to KNOW

- Following a severe crisis, things will never be exactly the same at your school. Everyone's expectations of education will have been violated forever.

- The activities of your school will eventually return to normal, but you must allow this process to unfold naturally while systematically continuing the crisis response in the days/weeks following the crisis.

- If the school was closed after the crisis, carefully plan your students' return to school. The Crisis Coordinator/head administrator should provide an opportunity for the school community members to visit the campus before classes resume. Have counselors available to provide emotional support during such visits.

- You might plan a special assembly/event at the beginning of the first day that students return to school after a crisis incident. The goal would be to help ease the students' transition back into the school environment and routine.

- *If the crisis involved the suicide of a school community member, see Section Eleven of this booklet, "Special Considerations for Suicide," for postvention guidelines.*

- If a preplanned special event (e.g., a graduation ceremony) falls shortly after the crisis, it is important that it not be canceled or entirely clouded by the crisis effects. Acknowledge both the continuing pain/grief and the fact that survivors have the right to feel happiness and other emotions besides sorrow after a crisis.

continued—

What You Need to DO

Who Should Do It: ✔ Crisis Coordinator/head administrator of affected school
✔ Custodial staff
✔ Campus Liaison
✔ Parent/Family Liaison
✔ Counseling Liaison
✔ Teachers
✔ Central office staff
✔ All crisis response team members

❏ If your school was closed after the crisis, reopen as soon as possible, preferably the day after the crisis incident. (If parts of your school building were damaged or sealed off by the police department, strive to find within 24 hours of the crisis incident an alternate location at which your students can gather. Don't be overly concerned with organization; the important point is not whether you have all textbooks and materials assembled but that your students are provided with the assistance of trained educators in processing their crisis reactions.)

❏ Do not significantly alter the school environment before the students arrive back at school. After the police finish their work, the custodial staff should clean up the worst of the damage (e.g., blood and broken glass) and make things orderly. However, do not delay the reopening of school for such repairs as filling bullet holes. (In fact, as explained later in this section, it is often best to leave these for at least a few days for public viewing.)

❏ Do not remove such evidence of the crisis as impromptu memorials (e.g., flowers, cards, religious symbols, etc.) created by school community members.

❏ Do not attempt to erase the presence of the crisis victims at school (e.g., by removing their personal belongings from their classrooms or by shuffling the desks). Such actions do not help survivors cope; they anger people.

❏ Prior to the students' return, the Crisis Coordinator/head administrator should decide the schedule for the day (i.e., whether the students will be expected to move with a normal bell schedule or whether that schedule will be modified to address the emotionality of the crisis effects). Any prescheduled after-school extracurricular activities should be held, but any field trips previously planned for the day should be canceled.

❏ The Crisis Coordinator and/or Campus Liaison should prepare the faculty for the students' reentry to school by holding a mandatory faculty meeting before school on the first and second mornings after the crisis. Provide time for the staff to express their fears/concerns, and review the plans made for assisting the students.

❏ The Crisis Coordinator should make clear to the faculty that they have permission to temporarily modify/set aside the regular curriculum to address the emotionality of the severe crisis/loss (*see "Modifying the Curriculum" later in this section for additional information*).

six

❏ When your students return to school, pay particular attention to the needs of those who arrive by bus rather than with the support of their parents. Arrange to have a counselor ride on each school bus on the first morning back to school.

❏ Have all the adults in the school greet the students/their families as they arrive. Post the adults outside, at the school doors, at the bus bays, and in the hallways. The intent is to reach out to the students and reassure them about their return.

❏ You might plan a special assembly/activity at the beginning of the day to help ease the students back into the school routine. After any such activity, students should go to their classes, where the school day should begin with a discussion of the updated crisis facts (*see "Telling the Facts" in Section One of this booklet for guidelines on appropriately sharing the facts with students*) and a processing session for the students. If the crisis was less severe, the processing sessions need occur only in the affected class(es). Or, if processing sessions already occurred on the first day of the crisis (*see "First-Day Task List" in Section Two of this booklet*), they can be shortened/skipped the next morning, as appropriate. (*See Section Five of this booklet, "Emotional Recovery in a Crisis," for information about the vital processing sessions that should be held at the classroom level.*)

❏ Work to nip "school phobia" in the bud by contacting the families of all students not in attendance to arrange a home visit. During such visits, the Parent/Family Liaison, Counseling Liaison, and/or members of your school's counseling staff should talk with the students about their fears and emphasize that they will be supported at school. Encourage the students to at least try a few hours at school, accompanied by their parents, before deciding they can't handle it.

❏ The Counseling Liaison should follow the schedule of all injured/deceased students and staff the first day back to school, as there will likely be extreme emotionality in their classes.

❏ Student input should be sought in deciding what to do with deceased victims' chairs, desks, and other items such as displayed artwork.

❏ If the crisis was severe, teachers should modify/set aside the regular curriculum for a limited time in order to address the emotionality of the situation (*see "Modifying the Curriculum" later in this section*).

❏ Provide individual counseling services to any students who have been significantly affected by the crisis (*see "Providing Counseling Services" in Section Seven of this booklet for guidelines*).

❏ The Parent/Family Liaison should send a note home to parents at the end of the day to update them on the status of the crisis and to reassure them that their children are being assisted at school in coping with their crisis reactions.

❏ Each day that your team provides a crisis response, the Counseling Liaison or the Parent/Family Liaison should make personal contact (by phone) with the parents of those students most affected by the crisis and/or those who needed individual counseling assistance during the day.

six

continued—

❑ After the first day (or two) back at school following a severe crisis, during which the schedule will likely be modified to help students cope with their crisis reactions, it is important to emphasize a return to everyday school routines. If some change in routine had been planned before the crisis, return to/maintain the previous schedule for a time to help provide a sense of security and comfort.

❑ On the second (or third) school day after the crisis, your school should, in most cases, be back on a normal bell schedule. Begin the day by providing any updated crisis information to the students. The Crisis Coordinator/head administrator can read this statement over the intercom or have the teachers read it to their classes. (*See "When Will Things Return to Normal?" in Chapter Six of the main* Coping With Crisis *book for a sample statement.*)

❑ During the second day back at school, teachers should gradually reintroduce the regular curriculum, taking their cue from the students.

❑ The entire crisis response team should meet at the end of every day during which you provide crisis intervention. Team members should compare notes about progress, plan the next day, and process their own reactions to the crisis.

❑ The Crisis Coordinator/head administrator should keep your central office (and, via the central office staff, the school board) apprised of the crisis response status.

❑ The Campus Liaison and Crisis Coordinator should reevaluate the school's need for outside assistance (*see "Help to Request During a School Crisis" and other related points in Section Four of this booklet*). The help of outside crisis responders can be beneficial even weeks or months after the crisis incident.

❑ The Parent/Family Liaison and/or Crisis Coordinator should return the personal possessions of deceased victims to their families when they are ready to receive them. The families can make an appointment to pick the items up at the school or the items can be delivered to their homes.

❑ Remove the deceased's names from your school's mailing list, automatic call machine/computer, guidance/school newsletter list, and any other "automatic contact" locations.

❑ Do not rush to erase the physical effects of the crisis (e.g., bullet holes), since many crisis survivors will likely want to revisit the place where the crisis occurred. Remove such physical traces only with the input of your school community, when the timing is right (i.e., at least three to seven days after the crisis, and perhaps longer; take your cue from the school community).

❑ When the police have released the crisis scene and the worst of the damage (i.e., blood and broken glass) has been cleaned up, allow students, staff, family members, and community members unlimited access (i.e., day and night) to the site. Have counselor(s) monitor the area to offer support to anyone overwhelmed by emotion.

❏ After a severe crisis, members of your school and the surrounding community will likely create a spontaneous memorial to the victims. Establish a certain area at the school for leaving flowers, etc., and hang block paper outside on which people can write condolence messages. (*See "Cautions Regarding Memorializing" and other related points later in this section for guidelines on permanent, planned memorials.*)

❏ Do not remove such memorial items without the approval of your school community. Consult with students and staff about the timing of this action.

❏ When these items are removed, place them in storage boxes at your school so that victims' families can have the opportunity to look through them and determine if there is anything that they wish to keep. Carefully review the contents before the families view them to ensure that there is nothing hurtful.

❏ In the days and weeks following a severe crisis, be alert for additional incidents that may cause trauma, such as bomb threats (common after school crises) and/or "copy-cat" crime threats (*see "'Copycat' Incidents" in Section Twelve of this booklet for information*). If such incidents occur, tell the truth about the threat and follow normal emergency procedures. However, be aware that in the days and weeks following a crisis, survivors are generally hypervigilant and fearful. You will likely need to provide a greater than usual amount of emotional support after any new trauma.

six

Modifying the Curriculum

What You Need to KNOW

- According to psychologist Abraham Maslow's hierarchy of needs, safety/security needs (e.g., the need to be safe from crimes/disasters) are preceded in importance to human beings only by physiological needs (e.g., the need for food, water, and shelter). All of these needs must be met before "higher order" needs (e.g., the need to learn/achieve) can be addressed. After your students' security has been threatened, they will not be able to pay attention to academics until their sense of security is restored.

- The Crisis Coordinator/head administrator should tell the faculty that they have permission to temporarily modify/set aside the regular curriculum to address the emotionality of a severe crisis or loss.

- Teachers should not force a "regular day" on grieving or traumatized students, but they also should not leave their classes completely unstructured. After a severe crisis, the crisis temporarily becomes the curriculum.

- Artwork, language arts, music, drama, and appropriate memorializing activities, as well as other types of alternate activities, are especially helpful when many students do not want to talk about their feelings/crisis reactions.

- Humor is important after a crisis, as laughter is a tension release for the body. It is helpful for students to find something positive and/or to make light of some (tasteful) situation during the day.

continued—

What You Need to DO

Who Should Do It: ✔ Teachers (and/or members of the school's mental health staff)

❑ Teachers of affected classes should shorten assignments, provide alternative activities that focus on the crisis, postpone quizzes/tests, and so forth, for a short time so that they can help their students cope with their emotions. They might focus on appropriate activities in the areas of artwork, language arts, music, drama, and memorializing activities.

❑ Drawing, painting, and the like, because they are "right brain" creative activities, are particularly helpful ways of connecting with one's feelings and expressing strong emotions such as grief and fear. Appropriate artwork activities pertaining to crises are limited only by teachers' and students' creativity. A few suggestions (*see "Modifying the Curriculum" in Chapter Six of the main* Coping With Crisis *book for complete details*) for facilitation by teachers and counselors follow:

- Having students draw the victims
- Having students draw themselves (e.g., during or after the crisis)
- Having an adult draw something requested by the students
- Abstract art
- Collage
- Clay
- "Safe Sanctuary" activity (from the book *Spinning Inward*, by educator and therapist Maureen Murdock)
- Sympathy cards
- Free expression

❑ There are innumerable language arts activities that can be helpful following a crisis. A few suggestions (*see "Modifying the Curriculum" in Chapter Six of the main* Coping With Crisis *book for complete details*) for facilitation by teachers and counselors follow:

- Reading passages
- Quotations
- Poetry
- Letters
- Journals

❑ Music is a potent force for recovery after a trauma, and there are many appropriate ways music can be used beneficially after a crisis. A few suggestions (*see "Modifying the Curriculum" in Chapter Six of the main* Coping With Crisis *book for complete details and song suggestions*) for facilitation by teachers and counselors follow:

- Intoning relaxation exercise
- "Entrainment" tape
- Humming relaxation
- Anger release movements to music
- Composing a song
- Singing
- Discussing song lyrics
- Playing relaxing background music

six

❏ The number and types of drama activities that can be helpful following a crisis are limited only by the creativity of the students and adult(s) concerned. Teachers might encourage the students to perform their own improvisations; expressing their emotions through acting—from the "safe" standpoint of the characters they play—may assist some students to identify and verbalize their crisis reactions. After a violent crisis, a drama class or troupe of interested students might wish to perform the one-act play *Bang, Bang, You're Dead*. (*See "Modifying the Curriculum" in Chapter Six of the main* Coping With Crisis *book for complete details and an Internet address to access the script of this play at no charge.*)

❏ If the crisis involved the death of a school community member, students may wish to memorialize the victim. Major or permanent memorials will require the approval of the school's administration (*see "Cautions Regarding Memorializing" later in this section for guidelines*), but there are some simple activities students can do as a class to help fulfill their need to remember the deceased. (*NOTE*: If the death was a suicide, the suicide victim should *not* be memorialized in *any way* because of the danger of suicide "contagion"; *see Section Eleven of this booklet, "Special Considerations for Suicide."*) A few memorializing suggestions (*see "Modifying the Curriculum" in Chapter Six of the main* Coping With Crisis *book for complete details*) for facilitation by teachers and counselors follow:

- Listing attributes
- Memory books
- Balloon ceremony
- Fund-raising (*see "Raising and Dispersing Funds" and "Student Memorializing Activities" later in this section for additional information*)
- Memory ribbons/other decorations
- Web sites
- Spontaneous memorials

❏ Teachers should provide a "standard" assignment for any student who does *not* wish to focus on the crisis, its effects, and/or his or her crisis reactions.

❏ The students' reactions to the crisis will come and go throughout the days following the crisis. Teachers should give permission for a range of emotions (even nervous laughter or seeming indifference) at all times.

❏ As for when to return to the regular curriculum, teachers should take their cue from the students. Eventually they will work through much of the emotionality and will be ready to pay attention to academics again. (However, teachers should not administer a quiz or test immediately after returning to the regular curriculum.)

Funeral Planning

What You Need to KNOW

- The family of the deceased will handle arrangements for the funeral service. While the school must respect the family's wishes, the Parent/Family Liaison or Crisis Coordinator should discuss with the family the specific needs of the school community members affected by the death and (gently!) make recommendations that will address the school's concerns. Most families are receptive to such input.

continued—

six

- The timing of the funeral is of particular importance if the death was a suicide. Because of the danger of suicide "contagion" it is crucial to avoid any sensationalism (*see Section Eleven of this booklet, "Special Considerations for Suicide," for more information*). Hundreds of students leaving school during the school day to attend the funeral serves to glorify the death.

- If more than one school community member has died in the crisis, the families might consider a joint funeral, which helps to unite the community and allows students attending the funerals to experience this difficult ceremony only once rather than numerous times over many days.

- If the service will be private, or if separate funerals will be held in the event of multiple deaths, you might encourage local clergy members to facilitate a community-wide memorial.

What You Need to DO

six

Who Should Do It: ✔ Parent/Family Liaison (or Crisis Coordinator)

❑ Recommend to the family members that the funeral be held after school, in the evening, or on a Saturday so that most parents can attend with their children and provide emotional support.

❑ If the deceased was a student, encourage the parents to consider purchasing a special type of unfinished casket upon which the student's friends/classmates can write good-bye messages.

❑ Ask that the family members pay attention to songs emphasizing hope for the future when selecting music to be played at the service.

❑ If the family gives you their permission to call the funeral home and/or clergy member, speak with the appropriate person about your recommendations.

Funeral Etiquette

What You Need to KNOW

- At an early age children have an awareness of and response to death. Students will likely wish to attend the funeral of a school community member.

- Students should be given a choice about attending a funeral. They should not be made to feel badly if they are uncomfortable with or frightened by the ceremonial aspects of death.

- Teachers should educate themselves about any unfamiliar funeral practices that may take place so that they can discuss them with their classes.

What You Need to DO

Who Should Do It: ✔ Teachers

❏ If students are to attend the funeral of a school community member, teachers should help prepare them for what will happen through classroom discussions about funeral terminology/etiquette.

❏ Teachers should encourage their students to ask them anything they wish about the death and the funeral. Teachers should provide honest answers in words the students will understand.

❏ *Teachers should consult the "Funeral Etiquette" section of Chapter Six of the main* Coping With Crisis *book for a review of funeral terminology they might wish to review with their students.*

❏ *Teachers should consult the "Funeral Etiquette" section of Chapter Six of the main* Coping With Crisis *book for suggestions about appropriate funeral etiquette they might discuss with their students.*

❏ If students plan to attend the funeral, teachers should encourage them to attend with their parents or another adult family member.

❏ If appropriate, teachers might suggest that students leave a special gift (e.g., a note or flower) near, on, or in the casket as a way of saying good-bye.

six

School Procedures Pertaining to Funerals

What You Need to DO

Who Should Do It: ✔ Crisis Coordinator/head administrator of affected school
✔ Counseling Liaison (and other mental health staff)
✔ Parent/Family Liaison
✔ All crisis response team members

❏ The Crisis Coordinator/head administrator should send a letter to all parents of students affected by the death/crisis. The letter should focus on the grieving process and encourage parents to talk with their children about the funeral and any memorial services, and to accompany them to those services if the students wish to attend.

❏ If the death was a suicide, provide information about suicide "contagion" and warning signs and encourage parents to seek immediate help if their children give any indication of suicidal ideation (*see "Suicide Postvention" and "Suicide Statistics, Causes, and Myths" in Section Eleven of this booklet for additional information*).

❏ The Crisis Coordinator/head administrator should release students to attend the memorial or funeral service if they wish to go. The students and their family members should provide their own transportation.

❏ Members of your crisis response team, administration, and counseling staffs should attend the funeral to pay your respects and provide support to students needing assistance.

❏ If it will not conflict with arrangements the family of the deceased may have made, provide a gathering space at the school and refreshments for staff, students, and their family members immediately following the service. (The Parent/Family Liaison or Crisis Coordinator should check with the family of the deceased before making any such arrangements.)

Cautions Regarding Memorializing

What You Need to KNOW

• After a severe school crisis (particularly one involving violence), your school community and members of the surrounding community will need and want ceremony/rituals to express their sorrow, outrage, and shock. Often, such activities involve memorializing the victims.

• A memorial promotes healing by providing an opportunity for community members to join together and participate in a ritual, and it brings closure to a period of grieving. School memorials send a clear message that it is time to move forward with regular school activities.

• Your school's administrators can both facilitate healing and ensure that the long-term needs of the school are met by guiding the memorial efforts of school community members.

• One of the most important (and difficult) rules about memorializing is that *the victim should not be memorialized in any way if the death was a suicide.* This ban is crucial to help prevent suicide "contagion" (*see "Suicide Postvention" in Section Eleven of this booklet for guidelines by the American Association of Suicidology that administrators can use to justify such decisions to family/friends of a suicide victim*). (The same policy should be in effect after the death of a school community member resulting from a high-risk behavior, such as driving drunk or an accidental drug overdose.)

• In cases when a memorial would be allowed (i.e., when the death was not a result of suicide or other high-risk/illicit activity), a "consumable" gesture (e.g., a scholarship) is always preferable to any sort of permanent memorial, such as a statue or plaque in a prominent location. If your school erected a memorial for every school community member who died, the school would eventually begin to look like a cemetery, because over the years a lot of bad things happen to school community members. When emotions are running high immediately after a crisis, it may be difficult to keep the "big picture" in mind, but you must be careful not to overshadow for years to come the focus on what goes on inside your building, which is learning.

What You Need to DO

Who Should Do It: ✔ Crisis Coordinator/head administrator of affected school

❑ If funds are donated to the school after a *suicide*, disseminate them to a worthy cause such as a scholarship fund or a suicide prevention organization rather than using them for any type of memorial.

❑ Consider memorials on a case-by-case basis when the death was not the result of suicide or a high-risk behavior. Exercise caution when planning a memorial, and consider (in addition to the cause of death) what your school has done historically to memorialize students and staff who have died.

❑ Do not rename your school in honor of a deceased school community member, as this would permanently link your school with the tragedy.

❑ Do not accept gifts from the families of victims without first discussing with them your policies on memorializing.

six

"Gift of the Tragedy"

What You Need to KNOW

- At some point after addressing the initial trauma, a community that has suffered a crisis will need to ask themselves, "What will be the gift from this tragedy?" This question asks survivors to consider what can be done to both honor/remember the deceased *and* to focus on the ongoing lives and needs of those who survived them.

- Sometimes the gift of the tragedy is intangible (e.g., a renewed appreciation for life or an organ transplant from the victim).

- The gift of the tragedy may be more concrete—that is, a permanent memorial. The best type of memorial to a deceased school community member is something that can be used by the entire community indefinitely and that enhances the lives of survivors. Examples from past school crises include the world-class soccer facility created in Butte, Montana, and the Stockton, California, Children's Museum.

- Other memorials pay direct tribute to the deceased. Particularly after a catastrophic crisis there may be overwhelming community support for some type of memorial that directly honors the lives lost (e.g., the memorial gardens honoring the victims of the school shootings in West Paducah, Kentucky, and near Jonesboro, Arkansas). Creating memorials that honor victims can be therapeutic for the school and community, providing people with a means of showing support and expressing their deep sorrow.

- Another kind of "memorial" does not honor the victims so much as it addresses the pressing needs of survivors. Making a dramatic change in the school environment (e.g., building a fence) after a severe crisis can be a way to facilitate feelings of safety and security for survivors.

continued—

What You Need to DO

Who Should Do It: ✔ Crisis Coordinator/head administrator of affected school

❑ Whatever your school decides to do to memorialize the victims of a crisis, you likely won't be able to please everyone involved. To meet the needs of the majority of those concerned, include in the decision-making process the school community members and family members most affected by the crisis. Encourage everyone to strive to reach consensus, and suggest a deadline by which a plan should be formulated.

❑ Take your time when planning any type of permanent memorial to crisis victims, and be sure to observe best practice guidelines for such memorials (*see "Cautions Regarding Memorializing" previously in this section*).

❑ Involve all appropriate school community members (i.e., staff, students, and family members) in the planning, design, and (if possible) the construction of any permanent memorial. Note, however, that it is important to establish who will make the final decisions about design, location, budget, etc.

❑ Carefully consider the location of a permanent memorial. It should be placed in a location where students can choose to look at it, but where it will not leap out at them every time they enter the grounds or building.

six

Raising and Dispersing Funds

What You Need to KNOW

• After a severe school crisis, government funds may be available to your school. These grants are usually earmarked for providing direct services to the school, such as funding intensive/long-term counseling for school community members. (*See "Financial Support Available in a Crisis" in Section Four of this booklet for a few suggestions about requesting and making use of such financial assistance.*)

• In addition to the possible fund-raising efforts of your students, others in your school and/or community (e.g., your PTA) may gather funds after a tragedy.

• Local corporations may make donations, and businesses may set out "collection buckets" around your town.

• If your school's crisis has been highly publicized, donations may also pour in from around the country and the world, as they did after the school shootings in West Paducah, Kentucky, and near Jonesboro, Arkansas.

What You Need to DO

Who Should Do It: ✔ Crisis Coordinator/head administrator of affected school

☐ Your school will need to determine a plan for distributing donated funds (as these are generally not used for direct services such as counseling). Always consider victims' needs first (e.g., using the money to help offset burial/medical expenses or to fund scholarships for adult victims' children). Remaining funds might be devoted to general scholarships (an excellent way to memorialize the victims and focus on survivors) or another memorial effort.

☐ Make the decision about how to disperse donated funds a joint one. It is recommended that your school form a committee of school and community members specifically for this purpose. Ensure that all key stakeholders are adequately represented.

Student Memorializing Activities

What You Need to KNOW

• Older students (i.e., middle/junior high and high schoolers) often feel a need to take some positive action in response to a crisis. When something bad happens in their school/community, they want to help in some meaningful way. If flooding caused the crisis, for example, they may wish to fill sandbags/collect blankets and food for survivors. If the school crisis involved the death of a school community member, they might collect funds for the burial or medical bills.

• These types of activities help students process the crisis by enabling them to assume some control over the circumstances and contribute to the crisis response.

What You Need to DO

Who Should Do It: ✔ Crisis Coordinator/head administrator of affected school
                       ✔ Counseling Liaison (and/or other members
                          of the school's counseling staff)

☐ Do not belittle the efforts of students to contribute, as they often do a lot of good.

☐ Encourage the students to channel their energy into positive actions and guide them in undertaking appropriate memorializing activities (e.g., fund-raising efforts).

☐ When students approach you with the idea for a project (or asking for ideas), make sure they are really committed to seeing it through before promising too much support. (You might wait to see if they return after your initial conversation. If they do, you'll know the commemorative effort is truly important to them.)

☐ Ensure that the students, rather than the school staff member assigned to assist them, do the actual work.

Memorializing by Parents/Other Community Members

What You Need to KNOW

- After a severe school crisis, parents and other concerned adults in your community (e.g., other family members of victims, emergency responders, politicians, etc.) may find creative ways to memorialize the victims and effect positive change in the community, state, or nation. They might, for example, form lobbying groups, testify before Congress, petition for pertinent legislation to be put on the ballot, form national foundations devoted to ending school violence, form support groups for survivors, or spearhead public relations campaigns.

- School representatives may or may not be invited to participate in such efforts. If approached, be sure to support the efforts in all appropriate ways (e.g., by funding, collaborating on, and/or publicizing them).

six

School Guidelines for Memorial Services

What You Need to KNOW

- Remember that if the death was a suicide, no school memorial service should be allowed (*see Section Eleven of this booklet, "Special Considerations for Suicide," for additional information*).

What You Need to DO

Who Should Do It:
- ✔ Crisis Coordinator/head administrator of affected school
- ✔ Counseling Liaison
- ✔ Campus Liaison
- ✔ Parent/Family Liaison
- ✔ Teachers

❑ If possible, conduct the school's memorial service within a week of the death.

❑ Involve the students and staff in the memorial planning, particularly those who were emotionally close to the deceased.

❑ Keep the memorial short (e.g., 15-20 minutes for elementary students, 30-40 minutes for secondary students).

❑ Include appropriate soothing music and student musical performances. (*See "Music" in the "Modifying the Curriculum" section of Chapter Six of the main* Coping With Crisis *book for suggestions.*)

six

❑ Include several brief speakers (e.g., school, district, city, and/or state representatives, as appropriate). Exercise caution in including religious speakers if yours is a public school. Also ensure that the speakers selected adequately represent (e.g., racially) all members of your school community and the surrounding community.

❑ If it is age appropriate to do so, include student representatives among the speakers to read a speech, a poem, or another tribute, or to sing a song. A school staff member should approve their selections and should talk to the student speakers beforehand about the emotionally charged atmosphere they should expect. Practicing their contributions will help the students to alleviate some of their anxiety.

❑ Strive to involve all of the students, not just those who will speak during the service, in some aspect of the memorial. For example, classes could contribute decorations for the gathering space or students could create memory ribbons to distribute before the service.

❑ You may wish to include physical symbols of life and hope for the future in the memorial service, such as flowers, balloons, and/or candles.

❑ The Parent/Family Liaison should notify the families of the deceased about the special service and/or memorializing activities planned by the school so they may attend. Do not be offended if attendance would be too painful for them.

❑ The Parent/Family Liaison and Crisis Coordinator/head administrator should make the decision about how much involvement victims' family members should have in planning memorials at your school.

❑ Teachers should prepare their students for the memorial service by explaining what will happen during the assembly and their expectations for respectful behavior. Teachers should remove any students who begin to behave inappropriately during the service. Note, however, that sincere expressions of emotion (e.g., weeping) should not be considered "inappropriate" behavior.

❑ Encourage all of the students (and staff members) to attend the memorial service at the school. However, attendance should not be mandatory.

❑ Some students may not wish to participate in the school memorial. Other students may not be able to attend because of parental objections. Be sure to provide a separate area/activity for these students, or dismiss them.

❑ Reconvene classes after the school's memorial service so that teachers and peers can provide emotional support to students. Teachers should accompany (or have another student accompany) any students who are experiencing intense grief to a counseling room for a one-to-one discussion with the Counseling Liaison or another member of your school's mental health staff (*see "Providing Counseling Services" in Section Seven of this booklet*).

section **seven**

Addressing the Trauma

This section outlines typical grief and crisis reactions of both adults and children/adolescents and then provides many specific suggestions for helping to alleviate crisis reactions through school counseling services.

Determining the Degree of Trauma

What You Need to KNOW

- The nature and severity of a school crisis will in part determine its effects on the survivors and community. Violence has a profound effect on people and is more difficult to recover from than crises generated by natural events. The number and severity of injuries are other significant factors.

- Past crisis experiences (whether similar in nature to this crisis or not) will heighten the crisis reaction. The level of support received after previous losses and tragedies will also affect the reaction.

- People can be severely affected by a crisis even when they are not directly involved in the event or close to the victim if they lack coping skills or have experienced a recent loss.

- Members of your school community may be more vulnerable to a severe crisis reaction if they have experienced any of the following in the past: relocation; death of a family member/close friend; significant loss (e.g., of a job, a cherished pet, a divorce); poverty; being the victim of a crime; serious illness; and/or suicidal ideation.

- In addition to physical injury and death, crisis outcomes may include psychological debilitation for many. But crises also present opportunities for personal growth and change. Crises bring unresolved issues to light, which allows people to work on problems (e.g., anger, substance abuse, domestic violence, etc.) that may have been previously hidden.

- Healing is an individual process. People may move back and forth between the stages of recovery after a crisis. There is no prescribed time after which an individual should "recover," nor is there one correct way to feel at any given time.

continued—

What You Need to DO

Who Should Do It: ✔ Counseling Liaison

☐ Answer the following questions to help anticipate the degree of emotional trauma for your school community following a school crisis or injury/death of a school community member:

- Who was the person killed or injured? Was he or she a long-time member of the school community? Well known? Well liked?
- What happened to the person? If he or she died, was the death unexpected (e.g., murder, suicide, accident)? An unexpected death and/or violent death will be more difficult to deal with than a death due to a long-term illness, for example.
- Where did the death occur? A death that occurs on school grounds will be more traumatic.
- What other tragedies have impacted your school, district, or community recently? The current crisis will cause other unresolved issues and emotions to resurface.
- Who was the suspected perpetrator (if an act of violence occurred)? If the person believed to be responsible for the injury/death is also a member of your school community, the level of emotionality will be much higher.

seven

Adult Crisis Reactions

What You Need to KNOW

- Adult reactions to a crisis often fall into the categories of panic and defeat. It is normal to have high anxiety and want to flee the scene. It is also common to feel that the world is very unsafe. Unresolved issues from the past may resurface, and it is not uncommon for adults to experience waves of emotion.

The following are typical signs of stress in adults after a crisis incident:

Feelings

- Sadness
- Anger
- Guilt/self-reproach
- Anxiety
- Loneliness
- Fatigue
- Helplessness
- Shock
- Yearning
- Emancipation
- Relief
- Numbness
- Hopelessness
- Fear/panic
- Deprivation
- Diminishment
- Embarrassment/humiliation

Cognitions

- Disbelief
- Confusion
- Preoccupation
- Sense of presence
- Hallucinations (visual, auditory)

Physical Sensations

- Hollowness in stomach
- Tightness in chest
- Tightness in throat
- Oversensitivity to noise
- Depersonalization
- Breathlessness/shortness of breath
- Weakness in muscles
- Lack of energy
- Dry mouth

Behaviors

- Sleep disturbances
- Appetite disturbances
- Absent-minded behavior
- Social withdrawal
- Dreams about the incident
- Avoidance of reminders of the incident
- Sighing
- Restless overactivity
- Crying
- Treasuring objects

seven

- Trauma throws people so far out of their normal range of equilibrium that it is difficult for them to restore a sense of balance in their life.

- Trauma is generally caused by acute stress, that is, stress caused by a sudden, arbitrary, often random event (e.g., crime, violence, natural disasters, accidents, acts of war).

- Following a trauma, all human beings experience a similar physical crisis reaction that is based on primitive brain responses designed to help ensure our survival. The body will first experience physical shock, disorientation, and numbness (i.e., "frozen fright") and then the "fight or flight" reaction. At some point exhaustion follows the physical arousal of "fight or flight."

- The three emotional stages of a crisis reaction are: (1) shock, disbelief, denial; (2) a cataclysm of emotions (e.g., anger/rage, fear/terror, sorrow/grief); and (3) a reconstruction of equilibrium (i.e., the "emotional roller-coaster" eventually becomes balanced).

- Trauma is accompanied by many losses for survivors (e.g., loss of control, of faith in God/other people, of a sense of fairness/justice, of personally significant property, of loved ones, of a sense of immortality/invulnerability, of a perceived future).

- Adults can mentally or behaviorally regress to childhood after a crisis.

Childhood/Adolescent Crisis Reactions

What You Need to KNOW

- Children's responses to a crisis/tragedy will vary by child and age but typically fall into these main areas: fear of the future; academic regression; behavioral regression; and nightmares, night terrors, and sleep disturbances.
- The following are symptoms of typical childhood/adolescent crisis reactions, broken down by ages:

Preschool (Ages 1-5)

- Thumb-sucking
- Bed-wetting
- Fear of the dark
- Fear of animals
- Clinging to parents/caregivers
- Night terrors
- Loss of bladder/bowel control
- Constipation
- Speech difficulties (e.g., stammering)
- Loss or increase of appetite

Early Childhood (Ages 5-11)

- Irritability
- Whining
- Clinging
- Aggressive behavior at home/school
- Overt competition with siblings for parents' attention
- Night terrors, nightmares, fear of the dark
- School avoidance
- Withdrawal from peers
- Loss of interest/poor concentration in school

Preadolescence (Ages 11-14)

- Sleep disturbance
- Appetite disturbance
- Rebellion at home
- Refusal to do chores
- Loss of interest in peer social activities
- School problems (e.g., fighting, withdrawal, loss of interest, attention-seeking behavior)
- Physical problems (e.g., headaches, vague aches/pains, skin eruptions, bowel problems, psychosomatic complaints)

Adolescence (Ages 14-18)

- Psychosomatic symptoms (e.g., rashes, bowel problems, headaches, asthma)
- Appetite and sleep disturbance
- Hypochondriasis (i.e., obsessive preoccupation with one's health, usually focusing on a particular symptom)

seven

- Amenorrhea or dysmenorrhea (i.e., absence of or disrupted/painful menstruation, respectively)
- Agitation or decrease in energy level, apathy
- Decline in interest in the opposite sex
- Irresponsible and/or delinquent behavior
- Decline in emancipatory struggles over parental control
- Poor concentration

• Young people sometimes express their emotions through "acting-out" behaviors (e.g., temper outbursts, being argumentative) or by behaving in a clingy, dependent, "immature" manner (including developmental setbacks). The most common signs of stress in children and teens after a crisis include the following:
- Crying
- Hyperactive or silly behavior
- Lack of emotional display
- Irritability
- Temper outbursts/tantrums
- Restlessness
- Misbehavior/acting-out behaviors
- Clinging to adults
- Unusual lack of maturity or overmaturity
- Being demanding
- Getting lost
- Changes in sleep/being afraid to go to bed by oneself
- Rambunctiousness
- Inactivity/lethargy
- Fear/worry
- Guilt
- Changes in appetite
- Changing one's physical appearance

• The most common crisis reactions of children and teens after a *violent homicide* include:
- Concern that the person suffered
- Horror from repeatedly visualizing the crime in one's mind
- Constant need to tell and retell the story of the crime
- Need to reenact the crime through play
- Desire to seek revenge against the murderer
- Yearning to join the loved one
- Questioning one's belief in God and/or an afterlife

seven

continued—

- Desire to plan one's own funeral (*NOTE*: This is a strong warning sign of suicidal ideation, and the student should be followed up with.)
- Fear of dying
- Fear of a loved one dying
- Fear of being left alone
- School phobia
- Nightmares
- Behavioral regression
- Inability to concentrate
- Exhibiting very aggressive behaviors

- A sign that a young child has been traumatized is "repetitive play"—compulsive, repetitive mannerisms (e.g., repeatedly zooming a toy car into a doll) that may or may not be a literal replay of the crisis incident.

Childhood Post-Traumatic Stress Disorder

- A severe crisis reaction, and/or a crisis reaction that appears weeks, months, or even years after the incident, might be an indication of childhood post-traumatic stress disorder (PTSD).

- A diagnosis of PTSD in children requires that the child has been exposed to a traumatic event in which both of the following were present: (1) experiencing, witnessing, or being confronted with an event that involved actual/threatened death or serious injury or a threat to the physical integrity of self or others; and (2) the child's response involved intense fear, helplessness, or horror (which in children may be expressed as disorganized or agitated behavior).

- The main symptoms of childhood PTSD are described as follows:
  - Reexperiencing the trauma during play, dreams, or flashbacks
  - Avoidance of reminders of the trauma or general numbness to all emotional topics
  - Increased "arousal" symptoms (e.g., startles easily, difficulty falling asleep or concentrating)

- The most critical determinants in developing PTSD are: (1) perceived life threat, (2) the potential for violence, (3) the experience of extreme fear, and (4) a sense of help-lessness. Sex, age, and ethnicity do not seem to be important in determining who might develop PTSD. Rather, the development of PTSD has been most related to the degree of exposure.

- Psychological predictors that put children at risk for PTSD include the following:
  - Ineffective ways of coping with stress (e.g., denial, passivity, avoidance)
  - Insufficient or diminished social support (e.g., from family, friends, and teachers)
  - Other stressful events happening after the crisis (e.g., parents separating/divorcing, parent losing a business/job)

What You Need to DO

Who Should Do It: ✔ Counseling Liaison

☐ *Refer to Chapter Eight of the main* Coping With Crisis *book, "Points for Parents," for suggestions to make to parents about how they can help their children cope with typical crisis effects.*

☐ *See "Providing Counseling Services" later in this section for suggestions about how school mental health staff can help address the typical childhood/adolescent crisis reactions of students.*

Immediate Trauma Recovery

What You Need to KNOW

- Most people find outside assistance helpful in dealing with a trauma (*see "Providing Counseling Services" later in this section*).

- Recovery in the days and weeks after a trauma is often affected by the severity of the immediate crisis reaction; the victim's/survivor's ability to understand what has happened; the stability of the victim's/survivor's equilibrium after the crisis; a supportive environment; and validation of the experience.

- Recovery issues for survivors include assuming some control of the event in one's mind; coming to an understanding of the crisis event and redefining values; reestablishing emotional equilibrium; reestablishing trust; reestablishing a future/new life; and reestablishing meaning.

seven

The Grieving Process

What You Need to KNOW

- Grief is the state of keen mental suffering over affliction/loss and of sharp sorrow, anguish, woe, and misery. It is most commonly associated with a loss due to death.

- The five classic stages of grief are: (1) denial, (2) bargaining, (3) anger, (4) depression, and (5) acceptance.

- Mourning doesn't end after a year. People require different amounts of time to work through these grief stages, and they might move back and forth between them. "Triggering" events can throw people back into earlier stages (e.g., anger) even after they feel that they've achieved acceptance.

- Factors influencing the intensity of grief include the relationship to the deceased; the age of the deceased; whether the death was anticipated or unexpected; whether the death was violent; previous trauma/losses experienced by the survivor; the extent of his or her support system; his or her religious beliefs; and his or her overall equilibrium/coping skills.

continued—

- Grieving is not confined to adults. Children also grieve, although they may do so differently than adults, depending upon their age and maturity. Children are resilient and generally handle death well.

- A brief description of children's understanding of death (or lack thereof), from age one to adolescence follows:

1 to 3 Years of Age

- Most concerned with how a death will affect their daily routine and needs.
- Use "magical thinking," believing that something they did caused the death or that they can bring the deceased back.
- Cannot differentiate between death and long-term absence.

4 to 5/6 Years of Age

- Do not view death as permanent.
- Due to this lack of understanding of permanence, cannot grieve as adults do.
- Have verbal ability but take things very literally (thus, adults should avoid using death analogies such as "going on a trip" or "going to sleep").

6/7 to 8 Years

- Begin to understand that death is permanent but believe it can happen only to the elderly.
- If a young person dies, may demand to know why.

8 to 10 Years

- Begin to understand that death is part of the natural order and that people of all ages die for many reasons.
- Understand that death could happen to them.

6/7 to 11 Years

- Children's growing cognitive abilities help them to think more realistically and understand the finality of death.
- May seek comfort in religious/spiritual beliefs and/or explore the scientific aspects of death.
- Capable of grief as defined by adults.

11 and Older

- Capable of understanding that death results when internal biological processes shut down.

Adolescents

- Should fully understand the finality of death by about age 13, but many do not. Adults should help to ground teenagers in the facts.
- Children of many ages (as well as adults) might experience a fear of "spirits" and "ghosts" associated with the death.

What You Need to DO

Who Should Do It: ✔ Counseling Liaison
✔ Teachers

❑ Following a school crisis that results in death, answer students' questions about death honestly, no matter what age the students are. However, provide as few details as are necessary to satisfy their curiosity and provide no graphic ones that may frighten them.

❑ When answering young students' questions about a death, think about how these students may interpret your words. (Young children, for example, often engage in "magical thinking" or the belief that their own thoughts/actions somehow caused the death.) Choose your words carefully.

Family Members of the Deceased

What You Need to KNOW

• When it is their child who has died, parents will likely experience several common bereavement reactions (*see "Adult Crisis Reactions" and "The Grieving Process" previously in this section*) and will likely experience them to a greater degree than if the deceased were another loved one. Because a parent's loss of a child goes against the natural order, the death of a child is possibly the most difficult loss to accept.

• Grief is a very individual process, just as each relationship between any two people is unique. There is no set time for grieving to end and no one correct way to feel at any given time.

What You Need to DO

Who Should Do It: ✔ Parent/Family Liaison (and/or Crisis Coordinator/ head administrator of affected school, Counseling Liaison)

❑ When speaking with family members of victims, you might talk about the feelings and experiences that are common in many people who are grieving in order to validate their emotions in this time of crisis. Also share suggestions for helping themselves and other family members—including surviving siblings—cope with their loss. (*See the "Family Members of the Deceased" section of Chapter Seven of the main* Coping With Crisis *book for all such information.*)

seven

Feelings of Guilt

What You Need to KNOW

- Feelings of guilt are quite common for people of all ages after a crisis/death. Often these feelings are irrational (i.e., the survivors had nothing to do with the crisis or could have done nothing better/differently than they did, but they believe otherwise). At other times, crisis survivors do have valid reasons to feel guilty (e.g., they had forewarning of the crisis but didn't take it seriously or didn't act).

- Feeling guilt does nothing to change the outcome of the tragedy and interferes with healing. Counseling assistance from a trained mental health worker is generally needed to resolve such debilitating feelings.

- Feelings of guilt after a crisis/death assume many forms, including "survivor's guilt"; confusion about causality (i.e., young students may think their thoughts/feelings caused the crisis); feeling one should have done more (i.e., to prevent/address the crisis); guilt that one was less traumatized than others; guilt about going on with life; guilt about previous conflicts with or negative thoughts about the deceased; and guilt for feeling some relief if the death came after a long illness.

seven

Typical Feelings After a Suicide

What You Need to KNOW

- When the death is a suicide, survivors will experience all of the expected grief reactions as well as some troubling mixed feelings. For survivors, grief may be accompanied by a sense of betrayal, guilt, and misunderstandings, for example.

- It may be helpful for survivors to think of death by suicide as a homicide in which the perpetrator is also the victim. They can then grieve and remember with love the "victim" while at the same time feel outrage and anger at the "perpetrator."

Providing Counseling Services

What You Need to KNOW

- We recommend that school administrators follow the advice of their school's and/or district's mental health staff about providing appropriate counseling services after a school crisis. Because these professionals have training in providing counseling services within the school environment, detailed points regarding counseling methodology are not given here. The following are a few suggestions about the organization and management of such services that will be helpful during and after a severe school crisis.

What You Need to DO

Who Should Do It: ✔ Counseling Liaison (and members of the
school's/district's mental health staff)
    ✔ Teachers
    ✔ Crisis Coordinator/head administrator of affected school
    ✔ Campus Liaison

Logistics

❏ As soon as is safe and feasible after a severe crisis incident, help get everyone back to their classrooms where they will be secure and accounted for.

❏ Dispense with requirements for parental permission for counseling in the midst of a crisis and in its aftermath.

❏ Evaluate your school's need for additional mental health practitioners to deliver an effective crisis response (*see "Help to Request During a School Crisis" in Section Four of this booklet*). Communicate your recommendations to the Campus Liaison and/or Crisis Coordinator.

❏ Reschedule the regular day's activities to meet the critical needs of your school after a crisis. Cancel *all* appointments and meetings that are not of an emergency nature, including special education meetings and testing.

❏ Set up areas for individual and group counseling, and clearly mark these areas with signs. Also designate a "friends' room" or "safe room" where students can go to talk to and support one another. Make a counselor available in this room for assistance if requested.

❏ Proactively reach out to all those who may need your assistance after the crisis: in classrooms, hallways and common areas, and on school buses.

❏ All members of your mental health staff can be of assistance even if they are not providing direct counseling services to students. Staff will be needed for many administrative duties after a crisis.

❏ Provide breaks for all staff and volunteers providing crisis counseling services. Establish a written break schedule and a break room with healthful beverages and snacks provided.

Counseling Students and Staff

❏ Follow the schedule of the deceased, as there will likely be extreme emotionality in these classes. Be sure to lead processing sessions (*see Section Five of this booklet, "Emotional Recovery in a Crisis"*) in these classes, and provide emotional support to grieving school community members there.

continued—

seven

❏ Target the following groups for counseling assistance first: (1) those who were injured in the crisis event; (2) those who witnessed the event in close proximity; (3) those emotionally close to the victims of the crisis (e.g., siblings, close friends); (4) those known to be at risk or to have suffered a recent loss; and (5) those known to have had a previous suicide attempt. These at-risk students might request counseling services themselves, or more likely, their teachers may refer them. In any event, list and locate those at risk and ensure that they receive counseling support (which may include pulling them out of class so counselors can speak with them individually).

❏ Communicate by phone with the parents of at-risk students as soon after the crisis as is possible, and keep in close contact with them over the following days.

❏ Most at-risk students will welcome the opportunity to talk about their crisis reactions. Utilize artwork, language arts activities, music, and/or drama with those who do not open up (*see "Modifying the Curriculum" in Section Six of this booklet for suggestions*). The day after your first communication attempt, again ask those students who did not open up if they would like to talk, and continue to stress your availability for discussion and emotional support. Follow up with all at-risk students in the days and weeks after the crisis.

❏ Help ease the transition of victims and suspected student perpetrator(s) back to school (*see "When Victims or Perpetrators Return to School" in Section Twelve of this booklet*).

❏ After a minor or moderately severe crisis, the teaching staff should be able to assist up to 95% of their students in the classroom setting. Ask them to refer any students in obvious distress for school-based counseling services.

❏ Have another student or a staff member escort these distressed students to the counseling area.

❏ Teachers should sign out students leaving class for counseling support and utilize special counseling passes for this purpose.

❏ Track the names (and total number) of students utilizing the school-based counseling services. Review these student contacts during your staff and/or crisis team meetings.

❏ Do what you can to give helpful responses to children's stress reactions. Some of the responses that school staff and parents can give include the following:

Preschool (Ages 1-5)
- Encourage expression through play reenactment.
- Provide verbal reassurance and physical comforting.
- Give frequent attention to affected children.
- Encourage expression regarding earlier losses of pets or toys.
- Provide comforting naptime and bedtime routines.
- Allow the children to sleep in the same room with their parents for a short time after the crisis.

Early Childhood (Ages 5-11)

- Respond to regressive behaviors with patience and tolerance.
- Conduct play sessions with adults and peers.
- Relax expectations in school and at home (with a clear understanding that this change is temporary and that the normal routine will resume when the children are feeling better).
- Provide opportunities for structured, but not demanding, chores and responsibilities at home and at school.
- Rehearse any safety measures to be taken in the event of a future crisis.

Preadolescence (Ages 11-14)

- Provide group activities geared toward the resumption of routines.
- Provide opportunities for involvement in same age-group activities.
- Conduct group discussions geared toward "reliving" the crisis and rehearsing appropriate behaviors in the event of a future crisis.
- Provide structured yet undemanding responsibilities.
- Temporarily relax expectations for performance at home and at school.
- Provide additional individual attention and consideration to affected students.

Adolescence (Ages 14-18)

- Encourage participation in any community rehabilitation and reclamation work.
- Encourage the resumption of social activities (e.g., athletics, clubs, etc.).
- Encourage discussion of the crisis event and reactions with peers, extended family members, and significant others.
- Temporarily relax the expectations for school and general performance.
- Encourage, but do not force, discussion of the crisis and its effects within the immediate family.

❑ Lead processing sessions for both the students and the school staff. The entire staff can meet together; student discussions should take place at the classroom level. (*See "General Processing Guidelines" and "The NOVA Processing Model" in Section Five of this booklet for instructions*.)

❑ During processing sessions, be alert for any individuals who are experiencing a severe crisis response and might benefit from individualized assistance. Speak with these individuals privately after the session.

❑ In the days and weeks following the crisis, be available to consult with and counsel staff regarding their crisis reactions as well as their concerns about their role in the crisis response and/or their students' recovery.

❑ Provide students and staff with permission for a range of emotions.

❑ Avoid religious symbolism and platitudes.

❑ Provide bilingual services, if necessary, and have counselors available who speak the primary languages (and understand the native cultures) of all affected students.

seven

continued—

❑ Review daily absentee lists to identify at-risk students who are absent. Follow up with these students and their families, making home visits as appropriate.

❑ Make a mental health referral for any student or staff member you believe needs individualized assistance from a private counselor. Then follow up within the next few days to ask if the appointment has been made. Stand by your recommendation. (*See the "Additional Assistance When Necessary" section of Chapter Eight of the main* Coping With Crisis *book for helpful responses to common reasons parents give for neglecting to obtain needed mental health assistance for their children.*)

❑ Consider the following guidelines when determining if an *immediate referral* should be made for the private counseling of a child. Make such a referral for:

- A child who experienced a trauma that was severe enough to provoke post-traumatic stress disorder (PTSD) symptoms in almost anyone.
- A child whose post-traumatic behavior is endangering himself or herself or others.
- A child whose reaction to the trauma includes threatening suicide, talking wistfully about being dead, or dwelling on issues related to death and dying.
- A child whose reaction to the trauma is so severe that his or her ability to differentiate between fantasy and reality is compromised.
- A child whose reaction to the trauma is so severe and overwhelming that his or her daily functioning is greatly disrupted and age-appropriate activities cannot be pursued.
- A child whose parents' depression or anxiety is so severe and debilitating that the parents prevent the family from reaching a sense of equilibrium and well being, no matter how well the child is recovering.

❑ Consider the following guidelines when determining if a referral should be made for the private counseling of a child *after six weeks*. Make such a referral for:

- A child whose primary focus of conversation and play is the crisis/trauma.
- A child who is easily overcome by extreme fear.
- A child who has regressed to the behavior one would expect of a much younger child and shows no signs of regaining his or her former skills and/or abilities.
- A child who continues to have severe sleep disturbances caused by the trauma.
- A child who exhibits a lack of pleasure in most routine activities or continues to be withdrawn or apathetic.
- A child who complains of illnesses or physical pains for which no medical explanation can be found.
- A child who continues to experience vivid terror in response to trauma-related sensory "triggers" with no decrease in intensity and/or frequency.
- A child whose behavior continues to have a negative impact on others.
- A child whose continued distractibility and lack of focus are inhibiting learning at school.
- A child who continues to blame himself or herself for the crisis or misperceives himself or herself as "bad."

- A child whose overall changes in personality are dramatic and anxiety provoking to parents and/or teachers.
- A child who exhibits reactions or behaviors following the crisis that are particularly upsetting to the child.
- A child whose parents' reactions to the crisis continue to be so upsetting that they interfere with the parents' ability to take charge of the family and establish a sense of normality.

❑ If you believe that a student needs private therapy, do not hesitate to recommend it out of fear that your district will have to pay for the treatment. (For a student who has an individualized education plan [IEP], consult with your school's special education supervisor.)

❑ Follow your school's and/or district's policies for making outside referrals (e.g., providing "x" number of names; at least two), but do not hesitate to encourage the family to go to a particular agency, facility, program, or private practitioner you are convinced would be the best place for them to obtain the help they need.

❑ Remember your professional ethics; avoid overinvolvement with clients (particularly children).

seven

Other Locations/Needs

❑ In the aftermath of the crisis, keep your school building open into the evening and during other times when it would normally be closed, and have counseling staff available to speak with those who come to the school for assistance.

❑ Have at least one counselor available to assist those visiting the crime scene/crisis incident location. Do not force conversation or assistance; simply be there to support anyone overcome with emotion.

❑ Have counseling staff available to assist family members after the family/community meeting(s) held at the school.

❑ Communicate with the counselors at other area schools so that they can provide assistance to any siblings/close friends of victims and suspected student perpetrator(s) at their schools. Also contact the counseling staff at "feeder" schools that victims or suspected student perpetrator(s) recently attended.

❑ Pair a counselor with any clergy member assisting your school.

❑ The Campus Liaison should provide all volunteers with guidelines for working in your school (*see "Making the Most of Outside Assistance" in Section Four of this booklet*) and should ask them to record the names of all students and staff with whom they work and their general impressions and concerns. The counseling staff should follow up internally on these recommendations.

❑ Members of your school's counseling staff should attend any funerals to assist students not accompanied by their parents.

continued—

❏ Provide extra counseling services at school the day of and the day after a memorial service or funeral. These ceremonies often provoke an intensified crisis reaction.

❏ Assist students with carrying out appropriate memorializing activities (*see "Student Memorializing Activities" in Section Six of this booklet*). Activities that are permanent, costly, highly ambitious, and/or may upset other bereaved school community members should not be initiated without the prior approval of the Crisis Coordinator/ head administrator and/or your school's crisis response team. Note that if the death was a suicide (or the result of another high-risk activity), no memorializing of any kind should occur. (*See "Suicide Postvention" in Section Eleven of this booklet for guidelines to follow if the death was a suicide.*)

❏ Meet with your colleagues/fellow crisis response team members at the end of every day your school provides a crisis response to process your reactions. Be sure to take care of the caregiver (*see Section Ten of this booklet, "Who Cares for the Caregiver?"*).

Long-Term Needs

❏ In the weeks after the crisis as well as near the one-year anniversary date of the crisis, follow up with all students who were referred for counseling services. Assign a school counselor/psychologist who regularly serves your school to keep track of which students require follow-up and when this contact has been made.

❏ Provide counseling services for as long as any of your school community members will benefit from them (e.g., for a week or month, until the end of the school year, throughout the summer and into the next school year, or even for several years in some extreme cases). Remember that an over-response is always preferred to an under-response.

❏ If the crisis was catastrophic, you may need to carefully orchestrate the beginning of the next school year.

❏ Because federal grants to fund extended counseling services are sometimes not received for months after the tragedy, these services may need to be funded locally and/or counselors' contracts may need to be extended. (*See "Financial Support Available in a Crisis" in Section Four of this booklet for more information.*)

❏ Eventually move the crisis counseling services to a less central or less intrusive location so that you can refocus your school on academics and hope for the future. Take the cue from your school community about when this move should occur, and make this a group decision. (Your school's and/or district's mental health staff, administrators, and crisis response team should jointly make such a decision.)

seven

section **eight**

Points for Parents

Chapter Eight of the main *Coping With Crisis* book, "Points for Parents," details practical suggestions for parents, other adult family members, and caregivers for effectively working with the school during a crisis and providing emotional assistance to students at home. The Parent/Family Liaison is encouraged to consult that chapter and provide parents with the information. Such information could be communicated to families individually as needed, could accompany a parent letter/Crisis Fact Sheet sent home, and/or could be included in the parent/family information packet distributed at the family/community meeting to be held at the school on the evening of the crisis. Be sure to clarify and supplement such suggestions with discussions with family members. Also be sure to provide opportunities for parents to ask questions about their children's recovery and the school's crisis response.

section nine

Community Concerns

This section broadens the focus from the immediate needs of the students and school community to needs related to the broader community. Included are suggestions for how the affected school can proactively serve in a leadership role in the crisis response within the community. In addition, the special needs of families of suspected student perpetrators are presented.

Your School's Leadership Role Within the Community

What You Need to KNOW

- During any severe school crisis, it is crucial for the school to assume a leadership role within the community. The school is a focus of the surrounding community, and it is natural and easy for parents and others to come to the school when they need information and/or support.

- School representatives should reach out to other appropriate agencies to open the lines of communication and facilitate interagency collaboration during the crisis response.

- It is essential that schools, law enforcement agencies, and juvenile authorities work together to ensure that appropriate legal consequences/interventions are implemented when a crime occurs on campus.

What You Need to DO

Who Should Do It: ✔ Crisis Coordinator/head administrator of affected school
✔ Central office staff
✔ Counseling Liaison
✔ All crisis response team members

☐ Any time a weapon (or the threat of a weapon, such as a bomb threat), drugs, or a potential crime is involved in an incident at school, it is essential to notify the police. If an action would be considered a crime if it occurred on the street

continued—

rather than on your school grounds (e.g., a physical fight resulting in injuries), you must contact the police. (*See "Summoning Police/Medical Personnel" and other related points in Section One of this booklet for information to provide to, and ways to work with, emergency responders during a crisis.*)

❏ Communicate closely with your central office about any serious incident that occurs. (*See "Alerting the Central Office" in Section One of this booklet for guidelines on involving your central office during a crisis.*)

❏ After you secure the safety of those at your own school and summon help, alert all of the other schools in the area (via the central office). Clear and expedient notification is important so that nearby schools can: (1) take safety precautions to protect their own students/staff, and (2) notify any family members/close friends of victims/ potential victims within their school communities. (*See "Notifying Area Schools" in Section One of this booklet for tips on quickly alerting nearby schools.*)

❏ After a severe school crisis, your school and central office should collaborate with community leaders (*see "Help to Request During a School Crisis" in Section Four of this booklet*) to plan the crisis response.

❏ In the event of a catastrophic, citywide crisis, all of the city's school principals should meet and communicate about the crisis as quickly as possible to coordinate the crisis response efforts by district. This collaboration is helpful any time a crisis directly impacts more than one school, regardless of whether the schools are in the same district.

nine

❏ Keep your school building open after the crisis and during hours when it would otherwise be closed (i.e., in the evening, over weekends and holidays) to position it as a source of support for your school community and the surrounding community.

❏ Hold a family/community meeting at the school the first evening of a severe crisis so that you can: (1) give everybody the facts and explain the school's crisis response plans; (2) provide a forum for school community members to process their crisis reactions; and (3) communicate to parents/other family members ways in which they can assist their children and themselves in coping with crisis effects. (*See "Why to Hold a Family/Community Meeting" and other related points in Section Two of this booklet for information about the meeting's format and content.*)

❏ The Crisis Coordinator, Counseling Liaison, and possibly members of an outside team assisting your school (*see "National Crisis Response Teams/Organizations" and "State Crisis Response Teams" in Section Four of this booklet*) should contact (in person) surviving victims and their families, and the families of deceased victims. You can be of assistance to these families in many ways, and, if the crisis occurred outside of school, an open dialogue with them will help you obtain the facts necessary to provide an appropriate crisis response at school.

❑ It is critical that you communicate with the family members when the death is a suicide, as there are some particularly sensitive issues in these cases. (*See "Suicide Postvention" in Section Eleven of this booklet and "Getting/Verifying the Facts" in Section One of this booklet for information about verifying facts with family members when a crisis occurs outside school hours and/or off-campus.*)

❑ By visiting the families of crisis victims, you also can provide a much-needed intervention with surviving school-age siblings that involves helping them to cope with their grief and process their reactions to the tragedy and working with their parents and teachers to gently transition them back to school.

❑ If the suspected perpetrator(s) in a school crisis are your students, contact their families as well to gently provide them with the known facts of the crisis, offer assistance, and provide interventions for school-age siblings. (*See "Families of Suspected Student Perpetrators" later in this section for guidelines.*)

Families of Suspected Student Perpetrators

What You Need to KNOW

- Families of suspected student perpetrator(s) will be dealing with painful issues with little support. As members of your school community, you should strive to extend these families compassion.

- Although perhaps a lower priority than providing immediate assistance to victims and their families, your school should make every effort to assist the families of suspected student perpetrator(s). Remember that they are still members of your school community and that their children have victimized them as well.

- Families of suspected student perpetrator(s) may not have the desire or resources to move from your community, nor should they be expected to. Those who remain in the community will have a difficult time escaping the effects of the tragedy, and you have a responsibility to any of the siblings attending your school to support them in making a fresh start and achieving to the best of their potential.

- The isolation most families of suspected student perpetrator(s) experience continues long after the actual tragedy, extending throughout the legal process, the sentencing, and beyond.

- The reactions of community members to families of suspected student perpetrator(s) derive from many factors, including the community members' religious beliefs; the severity of the crime; the motivations of the suspected perpetrator(s); the circumstances of the crisis incident; the actual/perceived culpability of the parents/family; public statements made by the family members; and the outcome of any criminal trial/sentencing.

- Blame of the families is more prevalent when the suspected perpetrator is a child, because parents are often considered responsible for the actions of their children.

continued—

nine

- In 42 states, parents are held legally responsible for the crimes of their children; in 17 states, parents are held criminally liable. Child access prevention (CAP) laws, which require adults to keep all firearms out of the reach of children, are the most stringent of these laws. Unfortunately, such laws are infrequently prosecuted.

- Even when the families have not been irresponsible with their guns, they are often still blamed by the public. These families may be harassed outright. It is not uncommon for them to receive hateful anonymous telephone calls.

- Some friends/relatives may "drop out" of these families' lives, shunning them as different.

What You Need to DO

Who Should Do It: ✔ Crisis Coordinator/head administrator of affected school
✔ Counseling Liaison
✔ Media Liaison

❑ The Crisis Coordinator/head administrator should call the parents of suspected student perpetrator(s) to personally tell them about the crisis and the suspected involvement of their children—if possible, do not let them first hear this news on the television or radio. Tell them whether their children have been taken into custody and/or to the hospital, and offer to have a school representative accompany them to the police station or hospital.

❑ Use the Crisis Fact Sheet to remind you to stick to the facts when you notify these families, and avoid using emotional language/terms. Because hearing this news will be traumatic for these families, you might follow the same guidelines when speaking with them as you would for providing an injury/death/missing notification (*see "Injury/Death Notification" in Chapter One of the main* Coping With Crisis *book*).

❑ Sometime before the family/community meeting to be held the evening of the crisis, the Crisis Coordinator, Counseling Liaison, and possibly members of an outside team assisting your school (*see "National Crisis Response Teams/Organizations" and "State Crisis Response Teams" in Section Four of this booklet*) should visit the family members of suspected student perpetrator(s) at their home(s) to provide condolences and to offer to convey any message the family members wish to send to the families of victims.

❑ The Counseling Liaison should make a mental health referral to assist the parents in coping with their pain and crisis reactions. If there are other children in the families, private family counseling would probably be helpful.

❑ Make every effort to assist the siblings of suspected student perpetrator(s) within your school. Be careful not to inadvertently punish them for the actions of their brother(s) or sister(s) by placing them in an alternative setting or otherwise stigmatizing them. Without a great deal of support from the school community, the prognosis for these siblings is not good socially or academically. In a high profile case, school administrators should discuss with the family whether the sibling(s) of a suspected student perpetrator would prefer to transfer to another school within your school system.

nine

❏ The Media Liaison should offer to "run interference" with the media for these families. If the families welcome the assistance, you could accompany the family members from the school—if they've arrived there—to waive off the media, and communicate with the families later in the day and in the days following the crisis incident. During that time, you could lend support and serve as a go-between with the media, sharing appropriate information/ statements from the families. (*See "Containing the Media" in Section Three of this booklet.*)

❏ Be discreet with the media, showing as much respect for these families as you would for families of victims and survivors. Do not release the names of the suspected student perpetrator(s) prior to family member notification. Do not provide photos of or personal information about suspected student perpetrator(s) without parental/family member permission. Likewise, do not provide the names of close friends or family members of the suspected student perpetrator(s) or personal information about such people.

❏ When speaking with the media, remember that it is important to avoid "glorifying" suspected student perpetrator(s) with excessive attention, which could contribute to future "copycat" incidents (*see "'Copycat' Incidents" in Section Twelve of this booklet for more information*). You might refuse to answer any questions about suspected student perpetrator(s), instead focusing on the needs of survivors and your school's prevention efforts.

nine

Who Cares for the Caregiver?

This section specifically addresses the needs of the people who are responding to the crisis: caregivers who are so concerned with taking care of everyone else that they might forget to attend to their own needs. Presented are some helpful ways for crisis response team members to take care of themselves so that they can work from a position of strength and be of the most assistance to others at school and in the community. (*NOTE*: The Campus Liaison might also photocopy and distribute these pages to any volunteer caregivers who provide extensive service within your school.)

Why Caregivers Need Care

What You Need to KNOW

- When you participate in the crisis response, you will likely be personally affected by the crisis and may need just as much support as victims and survivors.

- You may have had some training that enables you to control your own emotional responses in times of crisis, and you may function at a high level in spite of them, but they are there nevertheless.

- Issues pertaining to your own personal history of trauma/loss may resurface during a severe crisis, a process known as "counter-transference" or "vicarious victimization." These reactions can take you by surprise.

- When you become aware of the school crisis, you might experience an immediate emotional reaction involving fright, denial, anger, and/or anxiety/panic. You might feel unprepared to deal with the situation, but you are expected to help nonetheless.

- Over the longer term, the emotional effects of a trauma/disaster on caregivers, as well as victims and survivors, can be divided into four stages: the heroic, honeymoon, disillusionment, and reconstruction phases. (*See "Why Caring for*

continued—

Caregivers Is Necessary" in Chapter Ten of the main Coping With Crisis *book for more details about these phases identified by the Red Cross.)* The emotional/physical reactions and activities of these phases may last for up to several years after a severe crisis.

- Mental health workers who listen to victims and survivors discuss their feelings are at risk for experiencing "psychological burnout." Over time, some may become emotionally exhausted, callous, or derive less satisfaction from their jobs/caregiving role.

What You Need to DO

Who Should Do It: ✔ All crisis response team members

❑ Members of school (and even state and national) crisis response teams must remember to address their own crisis reactions. While your objective is to support others, you must also support yourself. You may think that you don't need any help, but if you openly and honestly attend to your feelings, you will likely discover that you have been affected by your crisis response role. Think about what you are advising others to do to help themselves, and take your own advice to heart.

❑ In addition to caregivers, people who are not *trained* as caregivers but who assume a "caretaking" role during a crisis may need some assistance in the aftermath of a crisis. Watch for such "heroes" in your school and community, and pay special attention to their needs to process their crisis reactions.

Positive Actions for Caregivers

ten

What You Need to KNOW

- If you, as a caregiver, are to be of help to the school and community, you must acknowledge and begin to address your own issues concerning death, trauma/loss, and crisis.

- You also must take care of your own physical and emotional needs throughout the crisis response and well beyond. You will likely also receive support from your colleagues or fellow crisis response team members and any outside crisis response team members assisting the school/community.

What You Need to DO

Who Should Do It: ✔ All crisis response team members

❑ Respect your limitations. Only you know your own history of trauma and loss and how those past events have affected you. Speak up about what you feel comfortable and uncomfortable doing. If there is something you just can't handle (for whatever reason), honor your needs and take on an alternate task. Discuss with the Crisis Coordinator any difficulties you may encounter.

❑ Ask your family to support you by lessening other pressures on you. If your family members are not being understanding of the demands the crisis intervention is placing on you, remind them that the intense crisis response generally lasts for no more than a few days. Point out that by supporting your work they are making a contribution to the crisis response and thus helping their community members.

❑ Don't forget to eat, even if you're not hungry. Also, stay hydrated by drinking lots of water. Be sure that someone is put in charge of bringing the team members and volunteer caregivers drinks and food that are easy and quick to eat and are healthful. A vitamin supplement (particularly a B-complex) might be beneficial.

❑ Take a break for a few minutes at least every two to three hours. Deep, "cleansing" breaths during these breaks will help to calm and reenergize you.

❑ At home, try to get sleep. Gentle herbal supplements (such as chamomile tea) may help you to fall asleep, as might warm milk. Avoid "sleeping pills," if possible, as you'll need to be sharp the next day.

❑ Exercise is a tremendous stress reliever. Try to find the time to at least take a brisk walk around the block.

❑ Avoid the use of alcohol and other drugs.

❑ Laughter is a stress reliever for the body and mind, and you would benefit from finding something humorous to laugh about with your team members/colleagues, no matter how tragic the crisis event is. Sharing a tasteful joke about something unrelated to the crisis does not make you an evil or insensitive person.

❑ Stick together, and support one another. In a stressful situation it is helpful to spend time in the presence of others who understand the stressors affecting you, such as your colleagues or team members. Gather informally at the end of the day to discuss your crisis reactions, and regularly process your reactions to the crisis with these team members/colleagues in the days, weeks, and months to come. If an outside crisis response team assisting the school or community offers a processing session for the local caregivers, be sure to attend.

❑ If you do not compare notes with your team members/colleagues, be sure to talk about your experiences with another empathetic listener (e.g., your spouse/partner). Although you might find it difficult to talk about your experiences to relatives and/or friends who are not directly involved in the same stressful situation, these people care about you and would like to understand what you're going through. And expressing your feelings to them will also help them to be understanding of any stress reactions you may exhibit at home.

❑ You might also gain some benefit from talking to a mental health practitioner one-to-one and/or your clergy member if you belong to a church.

❑ Retelling the story of the trauma (and your involvement in the crisis intervention) from beginning to end is an exercise that may be helpful to you.

ten

continued—

❏ Remember that those around you have been affected by the crisis as well. Be gentle with others in your family, at the school, and in the community.

❏ Recognize that your crisis reaction is a normal response when assisting others after a traumatic event. Give yourself permission to feel a range of emotions.

❏ Try not to second-guess yourself. Look at your crisis response efforts and the future of the school and community in a positive light.

❏ Don't panic if you have a flashback. They are normal after trauma and will decrease over time as well as become less painful. If flashbacks persist for longer than a month, speak with a mental health professional.

❏ Ask your supervisor for temporary relief from your everyday job responsibilities.

❏ Over the long term, maintain as normal a schedule as possible. Make routine daily decisions in order to regain a sense of control, and schedule your time to keep yourself busy. Don't make any big life changes for a while.

❏ Do something you enjoy in the days and weeks following the crisis. You are not expected to be sad every day.

❏ Remember your professional ethics. Caregivers in schools sometimes go overboard and become overinvolved with the children they are assisting. That is easy to do when a child has survived a horrible situation. Set appropriate limits on your involvement with the children you counsel. If you have any doubts about the appropriateness of your actions, discuss your plans with a colleague, a crisis response team member, or your supervisor.

ten

Special Considerations for Suicide

This section offers recommendations for responding to the suicide of a student or staff member. Suicide is the second leading cause of death for American children ages 11-19, and it is estimated that every four hours a child commits suicide in the United States. Yet few schools are prepared to deal with suicide effectively. All of the procedures for coping with crises presented in the other sections of this booklet apply following a suicide, plus there are some additional necessary steps that are outlined in this section. A school's crisis response after a suicide must be handled appropriately to *protect the other students*. One of the primary goals of suicide postvention is to prevent further suicides, as there is compelling evidence that children and teens follow the suicidal actions of their peers in a trend known as suicide "clusters" or "contagion."

Suicide Statistics, Causes, and Myths

What You Need to KNOW

- Warning signs indicating that a young person may be contemplating suicide include the following:
  - Previous suicide attempts or threats
  - Plans or attempts made to secure the means for suicide
  - Thinking or talking about suicide
  - Scratching, cutting, or marking the body
  - Risk-taking behavior (e.g., running away, jumping from heights)
  - Withdrawal from activities, family, and/or friends
  - Alcohol and other drug use
  - Neglect of personal appearance
  - Marked personality and/or behavior change
  - Persistent boredom, inability to concentrate

continued—

- Decline in quality of schoolwork
- Physical symptoms associated with emotions (e.g., stomachache, fatigue)
- Loss of interest in pleasurable activities
- Not tolerating praise or rewards
- Verbal hints (e.g., "I won't be a problem for you much longer")
- Putting affairs in order (e.g., giving away belongings)
- Becoming suddenly cheerful after a period of depression (which may indicate that the decision to commit suicide has been made)
- Prolonged depression
- Preoccupation with death and/or suicidal themes
- Destructive play or repetitive unrealistic play

What You Need to DO

Who Should Do It: ✔ Counseling Liaison
                   ✔ Crisis Coordinator/head administrator of affected school

❑ *See "Suicide Statistics, Causes, and Myths" in Chapter Eleven of the main* Coping With Crisis *book for numerous* statistics *illustrating the severity of the youth suicide problem in the United States.*

❑ *See "Suicide Statistics, Causes, and Myths" in Chapter Eleven of the main* Coping With Crisis *book for information about the most common* methods *used by youth to commit suicide.*

❑ *See "Suicide Statistics, Causes, and Myths" in Chapter Eleven of the main* Coping With Crisis *book for a list of* risk factors *associated with youth suicide, including the four most common precipitating factors that cause youth to follow through with plans to commit suicide.*

❑ *See "Suicide Statistics, Causes, and Myths" in Chapter Eleven of the main* Coping With Crisis *book for several of the more widely believed* myths *about suicide and the facts debunking them.*

eleven

Suicide Liability Issues

What You Need to KNOW

- The role of the school pertaining to youth suicide is essentially the following:
  - To detect potentially suicidal students (e.g., students who talk about suicide or write about it in a class essay).
  - To assess the severity of the risk level of the suicidal student. (School psychologists and counselors should have special training in this area.)

- To notify the parent(s)/guardian of a suicidal student. It is not enough to tell only the police. (It is good practice to document in writing that the parents have been notified and encouraged to obtain psychological assistance for their child within the community and to have two school representatives present when parents are notified.)
- To work with the parent(s)/guardian to secure the needed supervision and services for the suicidal student.
- To monitor the suicidal student and provide ongoing assistance. (In some states, if parents are resistant to obtaining needed psychological assistance for their children, school psychologists may provide services to suicidal minors without the permission of their parents. Check the statutes for your state.)

What You Need to DO

Who Should Do It: ✔ Head administrator of affected school
                       ✔ Central office staff

❏ *See "Liability Issues Pertaining to Suicide" in Chapter Eleven of the main* Coping With Crisis *book for details about these school responsibilities, with accompanying case examples.*

❏ After the suicide or suicide attempt of one of your students, consult with the district attorney to assess the potential liability of the school, staff members, and/or district.

Suicide Postvention

What You Need to KNOW

- It is critical that the actions taken by school staff after a suicide, which are collectively called suicide postvention, be handled delicately. The suicide of a school community member puts many others at risk for suicide, and specific, proven guidelines must be followed to help safeguard the student body. Of particular importance are the ways in which students are notified of the death and helped to process their reactions to it, the prohibition of any memorial to the suicide victim, and the identification and assistance of any students who may be at risk for suicide.

- After the suicide of a school community member, focus on two primary tasks: (1) assisting the students and staff in processing their reactions to the crisis, and (2) working to prevent additional suicides by attending to those at risk.

- We strongly recommend that school administrators follow the suicide postvention guidelines of the American Association of Suicidology (AAS). This 32-year old organization is recognized as the national authority on suicide prevention and postvention. A summary of its guidelines follows:
  - Don't dismiss school or encourage funeral attendance during school hours.
  - Don't dedicate a memorial to the deceased.

eleven

continued—

- Don't hold a large assembly to notify the school community members of a suicide.
- Do verify the facts and treat the death as a suicide.
- Do give the facts to the students (while downplaying the method).
- Do provide individual and group counseling (to address crisis reactions after a suicide).
- Do emphasize that no one else is to blame for the suicide.
- Do emphasize that help is available, that suicides can be prevented, and that everyone has a role to play in prevention.
- Do contact the family of the deceased.

What You Need to DO

Who Should Do It: ✔ Counseling Liaison
✔ Crisis Coordinator/head administrator of affected school
✔ Media Liaison
✔ Teachers

❑ Unless the suicide occurred at school, the Crisis Coordinator and Counseling Liaison (or another member of your school's/district's mental health staff) should contact the family of the deceased to verify the suicide (*see "Getting/ Verifying the Facts" in Section One of this booklet*). This contact should take place in person. Express the school's condolences.

❑ Either during this initial contact with the family or at a later time, do the following:

- Deliver any expressions of sorrow from students and staff who knew the suicide victim.
- Return personal items of the deceased student.
- Discuss funeral scheduling concerns (i.e., that school will not be dismissed for funeral attendance). (*See "Funeral Planning" in Section Six of this booklet for more information.*)
- Make a mental health referral for the family (particularly to assist surviving siblings).
- Discuss ways to assist the victim's sibling(s) at school.
- "Run interference" with the media, if the family welcomes such assistance.
- Emphasize that the school will maintain confidentiality with regard to personal details about the family.

❑ If the circumstances sound like a suicide but the family maintains that the death was accidental, a helpful term to use with the family is "suicide equivalent" behavior. At school, you should treat the situation like it may have been a suicide and address it accordingly. You can use the word suicide when talking with your students and staff (e.g., "We don't have all the facts and details but [the deceased's] behavior sounds very suicidal."), or you can use whatever language the parents request, as long as it does not conflict with the coroner's or medical examiner's ruling.

eleven

❑ To avoid glorifying the suicide, maintain the normal school schedule to the greatest extent possible.

❑ Create a Crisis Fact Sheet (*see "Telling the Facts" in Section One of this booklet for details*). Be sure to include on the sheet common warning signs of suicide (*see "Suicide Statistics, Causes, and Myths" previously in this section*) and sources of assistance in your community, including a suicide hotline number.

❑ Tell your staff and students about the suicide when the news is confirmed (*see "Telling the Facts" in Section One of this booklet*). It is important that the suicide be acknowledged and that your students and staff be given the opportunity to express their emotions and ask questions. Provide opportunities for students and staff to process (separately) their reactions to the tragedy. (*See all related points in Section Five of this booklet, "Emotional Recovery in a Crisis."*)

❑ School staff members can be notified as a group (but preferably will be notified individually before they arrive at school using your preestablished calling tree). Educate your *entire staff* (including bus drivers) about suicide "contagion" and postvention so that they will feel comfortable speaking with the students about the crisis and will be able to do so in an appropriate manner.

❑ *Students should never be given news of a suicide in an assembly format.* Tell them the news in groups of their own classroom/homeroom or smaller, preferably with their teacher and a member of the counseling staff and/or an administrator present.

❑ Tell the truth about the suicide, but provide no or few details about the method. Stick to the facts provided on the Crisis Fact Sheet.

❑ Do not spend time discussing why the person committed suicide. When students ask, a helpful response is: "We're never going to know why (name) killed himself/herself. We need to talk about you and your thoughts, feelings, and emotions. You have lost a classmate, and we need to focus on you because you're here."

❑ If the students ask, "Why didn't God stop (name) from killing himself/herself?" explain that there are many different beliefs about this question and encourage them to speak with their clergy members and/or parents.

❑ Do not glorify the deceased student in any way or communicate any approval of his or her actions.

❑ Emphasize that suicide is avoidable and that the deceased made a poor life choice.

❑ Do not portray the suicide victim as deviant or mentally ill. Instead, make clear that the victim had problems that were unique to him or her and "made a bad choice."

❑ Do not say, "There is nothing anyone could have done to prevent the suicide." Students need to understand that prevention is possible. However, emphasize that no one else except the victim is to blame for the victim's actions.

❑ During discussion of the suicide, focus on prevention (including recognizing warning signs) and explain that suicide is a major problem in our society.

eleven

continued—

❏ Emphasize the need to get immediate help for a suicidal person. Highlight the difference between "telling on" peers to get them into trouble and telling an adult in order to protect someone or save a life.

❏ Emphasize to students the help that is available to them at school and in the community. Post a local crisis hotline number in each classroom, and provide the students with a card/handout that lists warning signs for suicide and a crisis hotline number.

❏ The Counseling Liaison or another member of your school's mental health staff should follow the suicide victim's schedule to help the students and faculty in his or her class(es) cope with the death.

❏ If many students are upset, you may need to modify/set aside the regular curriculum for a short time in order to address the emotionality of the situation (*see "Modifying the Curriculum" in Section Six of this booklet for suggestions*).

❏ Upon hearing the news of the suicide, some upset students may wish to go home. In such instances, call a parent/authorized caretaker to come to school and escort them home. Give these parents/caretakers a copy of the Crisis Fact Sheet and encourage them to attend, with the distraught students, the family/community meeting to be held the night of the crisis (*see "Why to Hold a Family/Community Meeting" and other related points in Section Two of this booklet*).

❏ If a sibling of the suicide victim attends another area school, contact the counselor at that school so that he or she can provide emotional support.

❏ Send a letter home to parents to alert them of the crisis. Include in the letter the time and purpose of the family/community meeting to be held at the school that evening, and encourage the parents to attend the meeting with their children. Also include in the letter information about the danger of suicide "contagion"; the most common warning signs of suicide (*see "Suicide Statistics, Causes, and Myths" previously in this section*); and sources of assistance in your community, including a suicide hotline number. Urge parents to request help immediately if their children express or hint about any desire to kill themselves or exhibit any suicide warning signs.

❏ Plan and hold a family/community meeting at the school the evening of the crisis (*see "Sample Agenda for a Family/Community Meeting" and other related points in Section Two of this booklet for information about the meeting's format and content*).

❏ Provide counseling services to those close to the deceased (e.g., siblings, friends, teachers of the suicide victim) as soon as possible; these people will likely feel anger and guilt in addition to grief. (*See "Feelings of Guilt," "Typical Feelings After a Suicide," "Adult Crisis Reactions," and "Childhood/Adolescent Crisis Reactions" in Section Seven of this booklet.*)

❏ *If the media approach you, follow the guidelines presented in "Media Coverage of Suicides" later in this section.*

eleven

❏ Let any students and staff who wish to attend the funeral/memorial service know that the school has no objections, but do not dismiss school for this service.

❏ Teachers can help to prepare any students who plan to attend the funeral for what will happen there through classroom discussion (*see "Funeral Etiquette" in Chapter Six of the main* Coping With Crisis *book for guidelines*). Encourage the students to attend with their parents or another trusted adult.

❏ Follow the school procedures that would go into effect with the death of any school community member (e.g., flying your school's flag at half-mast). Do not try to pretend the death has not occurred.

❏ *However, do not memorialize, or allow the students to memorialize, the suicide victim at school in any way* (i.e., no physical memorial, nothing permanent such as a yearbook page, no dances/events dedicated to the deceased, etc.). Because of the danger of suicide "contagion," it is imperative to avoid glorifying or sensationalizing the death even indirectly.

❏ If funds are donated, allocate them to a worthy cause such as a suicide prevention effort or a scholarship to shift the focus from the suicide victim to the survivors.

❏ Administrators should have a copy of the American Association of Suicidology (AAS) recommendations to help them explain why this ban on memorials is necessary to prevent suicide "contagion." Call (202) 237-2280 to request a complete copy of *Postvention Guidelines for the Schools: Suggestions for Dealing With the Aftermath of Suicide in the Schools* (1998, 2nd ed.).

❏ If you ever make an exception to the memorial ban policy, do so only after a great deal of thought and planning (which should include the family of the deceased and those who were closest to the deceased).

Preventing Suicide "Contagion" at School

What You Need to KNOW

- To prevent "contagion" suicides from occurring, you must focus on two main tasks: (1) providing prevention efforts to those known to be suicidal, and (2) identifying others at risk for suicide.

- It is imperative to *take all threats of suicide seriously*. A student who writes or talks about suicide is at risk!

- School psychologists and counselors have training in suicide prevention and intervention. We encourage school administrators to follow their recommendations after the suicide or suicide attempt of a school community member.

- It is beyond the scope of this booklet to provide comprehensive procedures for suicide prevention and intervention efforts. A few of the most crucial guidelines are outlined following.

continued—

What You Need to DO

Who Should Do It: ✔ Counseling Liaison (and other members of the school's mental health staff)
✔ Campus Liaison
✔ Teachers

❏ Immediately begin "networking" efforts to identify and provide counseling assistance to two groups of students: those known to have been suicidal in the past and those who were emotionally close to the victim.

❏ The Campus Liaison should instruct all school staff to listen for any talk of additional threatened or attempted suicides among the student body.

❏ Designate a school staff member (e.g., the Counseling Liaison) that all other staff members should contact if they become aware of potentially at-risk students or suicide attempts. If *any* adult at school becomes aware of the possibility that a student is suicidal, he or she should immediately contact the designated school staff member, who will assess the student and/or refer the student for further assessment/treatment.

❏ If they have not already done so, your school's mental health staff should immediately familiarize themselves with the community resources available for assistance and establish a relationship with these individuals/organizations.

❏ Teachers should instruct their students to talk to *any* adult in the school community if they are concerned about the possible suicidality of a peer. That adult should then immediately contact the designated school staff member.

❏ You must *always* contact the parent(s)/guardian of a potentially suicidal student, regardless of whether the knowledge of the risk is firsthand or secondhand information. There are no exceptions to this rule.

❏ Contact the parent(s)/guardian every time information concerning a student's potential suicide risk comes to the attention of school staff, and document these contacts in writing.

❏ If the suicidal student's parent(s) are perceived to be "the problem," your professional challenge is to elicit a supportive reaction from them.

❏ Do not mince words with the parent(s) about removing guns/other potentially lethal instruments from the home of a suicidal student.

❏ Make a referral for the parent(s)/guardian of a suicidal student to a community agency or private practitioner with experience counseling suicidal youth. Within the next day or two, call the parent(s)/guardian to ensure that they have followed through with obtaining the recommended mental health assistance for the student.

❏ In the presence of a second school representative, ask difficult parent(s) (i.e., those who are uncooperative/angry/in a state of denial when informed about their child's suicidal intent) to sign a "Notification of Emergency Conference Form" documenting that they have been notified of their child's suicidal ideation and advised to seek

eleven

mental health assistance. (*See "Preventing Suicide 'Contagion' at Your School" in Chapter Eleven of the main* Coping With Crisis *book for a sample form.*) If the parent(s) refuse to sign the form, the second school representative should sign the form as a witness that the conversation took place.

❑ The parent(s) who refuse to obtain mental health assistance for a suicidal minor leave you no choice but to call your local child protective services agency.

❑ Communicate the following key points to the parent(s)/guardian of a suicidal student:
- "We have assessed the suicide risk and had your child sign a 'No-Suicide Contract.'" (*See "Preventing Suicide 'Contagion' at Your School" in Chapter Eleven of the main* Coping With Crisis *book for a sample contract.*)
- "A local crisis hotline number was provided to your child." (Give the parent[s]/guardian the number as well.)
- "We need you to work cooperatively with us to assist your child. It is important that you follow our intervention advice and act on the mental health referral we provide." (Depending upon the severity level of the suicide risk, your intervention recommendations will range from immediate hospitalization to outpatient treatment.)
- "If your child refuses to see the mental health professional, you must insist that he or she does so and accompany your child to the appointments." (Explain to the parent[s]/guardian that you can assist in convincing the child to attend the sessions, if necessary.)
- "For your child's sake, you must recognize the seriousness of this problem and act quickly."
- "You need to focus on your child's needs now. Providing him/her with assistance must be a priority in your family."
- "It is important that you increase your supervision and emotional support of your child." (A critical child should not, for example, come home to an empty house after school.)
- "Immediately remove any guns and other potentially lethal instruments (e.g., knives, ropes, prescription medications) from your home. Telling your child not to touch your gun is not good enough!"
- "Be patient with your child. Try not to be angry with him/her because of the suicidal intent."
- "Offer to help your child with 'no strings attached.'"
- "Keep communication going with your child and try to prevent him/her from feeling isolated. Enlist the assistance of your family members and trusted family friends to interact with your child."
- "Show your child love, acceptance, and tolerance. This is not the time to 'get tough.'"
- "Take all suicidal threats and attempts seriously. If you believe suicide threats are attention-seeking and manipulative behaviors, then allow yourself to be manipulated!"

eleven

continued—

❏ The school's mental health staff should follow these key points when interacting with suicidal students:

- Try to remain calm, and seek collaboration from a colleague.

- Gather case history information from the student. Asking the student questions as if he or she were planning a "trip" rather than a suicide can help to elicit concrete facts about the plans and alleviate some anxiety on your part. (For example, you might ask, "How long have you been planning this?" "Who have you told about these plans?" "Are you planning to take anyone else with you?" and so forth.)

- Ask specific questions about the suicide plan and the frequency and duration of suicidal thoughts. The most important question for the student to answer is, "How would you end your life?" The student's answer to that question will in large part help you determine the severity of the risk and guide your next steps.

- Emphasize that there are alternatives to suicide and that the student is not the first person to feel this way.

- Do not agree to keep the student's suicidal thoughts or actions a secret. Explain your ethical responsibility to notify his or her parent(s)/guardian.

- Ask the student to sign a "No-Suicide Contract" (*see "Preventing Suicide 'Contagion' at Your School" in Chapter Eleven of the main* Coping With Crisis *book for a sample contract*).

- Provide the student with the phone number of the local crisis hotline.

- Supervise the student until his or her parent(s)/guardian have assumed responsibility.

- Make a follow-up appointment at school with the suicidal student.

Suicide Attempts

What You Need to DO

eleven

Who Should Do It: ✔ Counseling Liaison
✔ Crisis Coordinator/head administrator of affected school

❏ If a student attempts suicide at your school, immediately call for professional medical/mental health assistance.

❏ Remove all potentially lethal weapons/instruments from the student and his or her immediate area, if it is possible to do so without jeopardizing your physical safety.

❏ Closely supervise the student until professional assistance arrives, including physically restraining the student if he or she poses a threat of imminent physical harm to himself or herself.

❏ Negotiate with the student, if necessary, but do not promise to withhold information about the suicide attempt from his or her parent(s)/guardian. Treat the student gently and with respect, and stay calm. Grant the student's immediate requests, such as to see a favorite teacher or other support person.

❏ Notify the student's parent(s)/guardian.

❏ Help those in your school community who become aware of the attempt, and preferably your entire student body, to process their reactions to the crisis. (*See "Suicide Postvention" previously in this section for guidelines.*)

❏ If your school has not been notified of a suicide attempt made off school grounds, but members of your student body are discussing such an incident, contact the family of the potential suicide victim to verify the rumor. The Crisis Coordinator and/or Counseling Liaison should speak with the family in person. Making this contact may be uncomfortable, but you must obtain the facts so that you can provide an appropriate intervention for the student and your school community as a whole. (*See "Suicide Postvention" previously in this section for guidelines.*)

❏ If the parent(s)/guardian of the potential suicide victim are unaware of the rumored suicide attempt, discuss with the parent(s)/guardian the student's risk for suicide (*see "Preventing Suicide 'Contagion' at School" previously in this section for guidelines*).

Media Coverage of Suicides

What You Need to KNOW

- Some research shows that media coverage of a suicide can be a causal factor in suicide "contagion"/"clusters."

- Because youth suicide is so common, an isolated suicide at your school may not be considered newsworthy by the media unless yours is a small community, there was a suicide "cluster" in one geographical area, or there was a "pact" between students who committed suicide together.

- All of the guidelines presented previously for dealing with the media after a school crisis (*see especially Section Three of this booklet, "Here Come the Media"*) apply after a suicide, with a few additional points specific to this type of school crisis.

- The school spokesperson granting the media interview(s) after a suicide should have a thorough understanding of the dynamics of youth suicide. If the Media Liaison does *not* possess this knowledge, someone from your school's/district's mental health staff should conduct the interview(s) instead of/in collaboration with the Media Liaison.

- To prevent suicide "contagion," it is critical that the suicide not be portrayed as a tragic, heroic, romantic, or mystical response to stress/life's pressures.

- After a suicide, it is particularly important to convey a cooperative demeanor with the media because: (1) you will want to positively influence media coverage (if any) of the tragedy; (2) your school is the first place the media will come for information; and (3) your school will be closely linked with the suicide victim in the media coverage.

eleven

continued—

What You Need to DO

Who Should Do It: ✔ Media Liaison (and/or a member of your school's/district's mental health staff)

❑ If contacted by the media, do not refuse to give an interview and do not simply read a prepared statement.

❑ Avoid becoming defensive with the media.

❑ Remember the valuable role the media can play in disseminating to the public important information about suicide warning signs and sources of assistance.

❑ Encourage the media not to cover the story. Suggest, instead, that they come back in a few weeks to do a story on suicide prevention.

❑ Honestly acknowledge the suicide or "suicide equivalent" action (*see "Suicide Postvention" previously in this section*).

❑ Provide brief identifying information about the victim such as age, grade, and gender. Obtain parental permission prior to releasing the name of the victim, even if other sources (e.g., the police) are already reporting the student's name.

❑ Answer the media's questions, but protect confidential information about the victim and his or her family.

❑ Avoid discussion of the circumstances/causation of the suicide and details of the victim's life.

❑ Do not provide details about the method of suicide.

❑ Read any statement provided by the victim's family. (Edit this statement, if necessary, to ensure that it complies with the guidelines of the American Association of Suicidology, or refuse to read it. *See "Suicide Postvention" previously in this section for additional information on the AAS guidelines.*)

❑ Express the sorrow of the school staff and student body.

❑ Emphasize the steps your school is taking to assist the other students in coping with the suicide, including the counseling services available within the school and the community. Explain that the students are being encouraged to continue with their normal school activities to the greatest extent possible.

❑ Publicize the time of the family/community meeting to be held at the school the evening of the crisis (*see "Why to Hold a Family/Community Meeting" and other related points in Section Two of this booklet*), and encourage all concerned parents to attend with their children.

❑ Acknowledge the widespread problem of youth suicide, citing appropriate statistics (*see "Suicide Statistics, Causes, and Myths" in Chapter Eleven of the main* Coping With Crisis *book for details*).

eleven

❑ Emphasize any suicide prevention efforts your school/district has previously implemented, and provide documentation.

❑ Ask the media to emphasize the warning signs of suicide (*see "Suicide Statistics, Causes, and Myths" previously in this section*) and sources of assistance both at the school and in the community.

❑ Explain to the media the suicide "contagion"/"clusters" phenomenon and ask them to follow the media guidelines of the American Association of Suicidology (AAS) in their coverage. A summary of these guidelines follows:

- Avoid details of the method.
- Do not report the suicide as unexplainable or the result of simplistic or romantic causes.
- Avoid making the story front-page news and avoid the word "suicide" in the headline.
- Do not print a photograph of the deceased.
- Refrain from coverage that excites or sensationalizes.
- Do not imply approval of suicide.
- Use simple language and review all statistics to ensure that accurate information is conveyed. Cite sources when appropriate.
- Be cautious about contacting the survivors of a suicide victim or a person who has attempted suicide. It is preferable to have the school obtain approval from such people prior to your contact (if any).
- Avoid discussing the specifics of the situation and safeguard confidential information about the victim and his or her family.
- Include, if possible, positive outcomes of suicidal crises. (That is, coverage of those who contemplated suicide but decided against it or received assistance would be more appropriate.)
- Include information on the warning signs, sources of help, and what one should do if one becomes aware that someone is suicidal.

eleven

section twelve

Is It Over?

Soon after you provide the initial crisis response (i.e., in the hours, days, and/or the first few weeks following a severe crisis incident), it will be important to turn your attention to the future. As you address the "fallout" of the crisis, you may want to make some changes in your school building and/or crisis response policies. During this time, you must also stay alert for additional crises happening in the wake of the initial crisis, address the long-term counseling needs of school community members, and prepare for possible litigation resulting from the crisis incident.

Team Regrouping After a Crisis

What You Need to KNOW

- Planning for the future and refining your crisis response procedures is important, because there *will* be another crisis of some type at your school in the future.

What You Need to DO

Who Should Do It:
✔ Crisis Coordinator/head administrator of affected school
✔ Central office staff
✔ All crisis response team members

❏ Once you have had time to reflect upon the crisis and crisis response, schedule at least one "regrouping" meeting with your team and the leaders from your school/district. Allow enough time for a lengthy, uninterrupted discussion.

❏ Document—either by tape recorder or with very thorough notes—the discussion at this meeting.

❏ Discuss how your team members are recovering from the effects of the crisis; what worked well in terms of the crisis response; and what didn't go well during the crisis. List the problems in writing. (Do not, however, make this discussion a forum for blame and criticism. Each member of your team did the best he or she could do at the time and needs your support.)

continued—

❏ Make each problem listed an action item. Assign responsibility for rectifying each problem to either an individual or a committee and determine a reasonable time frame for completion. Then follow up.

❏ Discuss any root causes that may have contributed to the crisis incident.

❏ Discuss what you might do to begin to resolve some of these factors and/or improve the climate of your school. Brainstorm actions appropriate for your school and make a concrete plan to implement the most feasible ideas.

❏ For any major decisions, be sure to solicit the input of everyone who will be affected by the plan (i.e., staff members, students, and parents). Participation breeds "ownership."

❏ Schedule a meeting to share your experience and what you have learned from the crisis with the other schools in your district so that they might learn from your example and be better prepared when faced with their own crises.

❏ If your school's crisis was catastrophic, you might consult with your state's department of education and/or the state police to create a statewide inservice program on crisis response.

"Copycat" Incidents

What You Need to KNOW

- Both adults and children have committed atrocious "copycat" acts after hearing of tragedies elsewhere.

- Some perpetrators seem to copy violent acts depicted in movies and television programs.

- News coverage of violent acts can give already troubled children some specific ideas about actions that they could take in *their* communities.

- The media coverage of suspected student perpetrators may excite children, who are both impressionable and attention seekers. Some children may be envious of the attention paid to the perpetrators of violence and seek to gain some attention for themselves by imitating their actions.

- Following a severe crisis at your school or at another nearby school, anticipate the occurrence of additional crises. Bomb threats are quite common, and students sometimes threaten to continue or "finish" the violent/destructive actions of suspected student perpetrators. If a crisis was nationally publicized, schools throughout the country should be on the alert for signs of a "copycat."

twelve

What You Need to DO

Who Should Do It: ✔ Crisis Coordinator/head administrator of affected school
✔ All crisis response team members
✔ Central office staff
✔ Teachers

❑ Prepare for "copycat" threats and/or incidents by heightening security and *taking any threats at your school very seriously.*

❑ Implement the following procedures to prepare your school for any "copycat" threats you may receive:

- Review your school's crisis response plan, and organize (or keep on "standby") your crisis response team.

- Alert all of your school staff that in the next few days your school may experience bomb threats; violent, attention-seeking actions by students; and imitations of the suspected student perpetrator(s)' dress and/or actions.

- Instruct all of your school staff to immediately report any threats of violence or violent actions, both past and present. Fully investigate all such threats.

- Whenever possible, provide extra security rather than canceling school. Take every precaution necessary (e.g., temporarily checking student backpacks or posting security guards) to protect human safety while at the same time striving to maintain the regular schedule and a calm atmosphere.

- *See "Less Severe Crises" in Chapter One of the main* Coping With Crisis *book for recommended procedures to follow in the event of a bomb threat.*

- Involve the police in a timely manner whenever a crime is committed or is threatened. Follow their instructions.

- Communicate closely with your central office in the event of any threat or crime, as central administration staff may wish to become involved in the crisis response or may need to alert other area schools.

- Make your school administrators, security staff, and teachers extra visible (e.g., positioning them in the hallways and common areas) in the days following a publicized severe crisis or "copycat" threat. The dual goals are to restore a sense of safety within the school and to watch and listen for any potential "copycats."

- Have all teachers explain to their students (e.g., by reading a statement from the head administrator) that the school is taking all necessary steps to protect their safety. Emphasize how important it is for students to immediately report to an adult in the school any rumors/threats of violence and that all such threats will be investigated. Also tell students that any academic time lost due to bomb (or other) threats will be made up during a student holiday or in the summer, as necessary.

- Communicate to parents any extra security measures taken through a home letter. The purpose of the letter is to control rumors about any "copycat" threats and to reassure parents about the safety of their children at school. Encourage normal school attendance.

twelve

continued—

☐ Children and teens often follow the suicidal actions of their peers, a trend known as suicide "clusters" or "contagion." If a suicide occurs in your school community, monitor closely any at-risk students and be alert for suicide threats among students. (*See "Suicide Postvention" in Section Eleven of this booklet for guidelines on handling appropriately the aftereffects of a suicide within the school community.*)

☐ Also send a note home to parents notifying them that there has been a suicide within the school community and explaining to them the potential for suicide "contagion." Encourage parents to request help immediately if their children hint about or express any desire to kill themselves.

Long-Term Emotional Effects

What You Need to KNOW

- How long it will take the people in your school and community to recover from a crisis will depend, in part, upon its severity and how effective the initial crisis response was. If your school crisis was severe, you can anticipate addressing its effects for many weeks, months, or even years to come.

- Not all victims/survivors of a crisis suffer from long-term stress reactions, but many do. It is natural for those who have experienced a trauma to continue to reexperience crisis reactions over long periods of time.

- Long-term crisis reactions may be made worse by the actions or reactions of others. When the reactions of others are sensed to be negative (whether this was intentional or not), they are called the "second assault," and the associated feelings for the victim are described as a "second injury."

- After some crises, educators have been sources of a "second assault." To prevent that from happening at your school, encourage everyone to respond to victims/survivors experiencing long-term stress reactions with sensitivity and patience.

twelve

- If school administrators do not make the continued emotional support of the staff a priority, the school may lose some valuable educators. Teachers (and administrators) whose sense of security has been violated to a severe degree may lose their faith in education and change careers or take early retirement.

- Crisis reactions that victims/survivors may experience in the long term include all those they felt immediately following the crisis (*see "Adult Crisis Reactions" and "Childhood/Adolescent Crisis Reactions" in Section Seven of this booklet for details*) as well as other new or intensified reactions such as substance abuse or post-traumatic stress disorder (PTSD).

- Post-traumatic stress disorder (PTSD) requires professional mental health treatment to diagnose and resolve. (*See "Long-Term Effects" in Chapter Twelve of the main* Coping With Crisis *book for a clinical description of PTSD symptoms.*)

- A victim's/survivor's stress reactions warrant private treatment if they persist in a severe form for longer than a month.

What You Need to DO

Who Should Do It: ✔ Counseling Liaison (and other members of your school's/district's mental health staff)
✔ Campus Liaison
✔ Teachers
✔ Parent/Family Liaison
✔ Crisis Coordinator/head administrator of affected school
✔ Central office staff
✔ All crisis response team members

❑ Provide ongoing opportunities for the staff to express their concerns and process their long-term reactions to the crisis (*see Section Five of this booklet, "Emotional Recovery in a Crisis"*).

❑ Familiarize your staff members with post-traumatic stress reactions so that they can better support the students and one another. Your crisis response team, as well as others from your school's/district's mental health staff, could communicate this information, or you might utilize the assistance of people specially trained in crisis response from outside your school/district. (*See "Help to Request During a School Crisis" in Section Four of this booklet for suggestions.*) Note that if the school crisis was catastrophic, training in post-traumatic stress reactions should take place on a district-wide/citywide basis, as the long-term effects of the crisis will be far reaching.

❑ The Counseling Liaison and other members of the mental health staff should provide ongoing support to school community members and assist them in dealing with their and their students' normal long-term crisis reactions by:
  - Respecting and fulfilling their continued need to discuss the crisis incident.
  - Letting students know there will continue to be people who are willing to listen to them.
  - Providing students with responsible, trained adult "listeners."
  - Anticipating delayed effects and identifying "triggers" of those crisis effects (*see "Anniversaries and Significant Dates" later in this section*).
  - Watching for pathological long-term stress reactions.

❑ Also support your students by communicating with their parents. The Parent/Family Liaison should send a letter home approximately one month after a severe crisis explaining long-term crisis effects and providing guidelines for identifying pathological crisis reactions.

❑ Identify students experiencing long-term difficulties and follow up with these students' parents, making referrals for private counseling as appropriate.

twelve

continued—

❏ Continue to provide counseling services to students for weeks, months, or even into the next school year, depending upon the severity of the crisis. (*See "Providing Counseling Services" in Section Seven of this booklet for guidelines.*)

❏ Eventually you may want to deemphasize the location of the counseling services provided within your school building or relocate them, helping to regain a sense of normalcy. Take your cue from the student body and staff regarding the timing of this change.

❏ Very young children who survive a crisis and/or lose a loved one during a school crisis will need ongoing assistance to understand what has happened. (*See "Childhood/ Adolescent Crisis Reactions" in Section Seven of this booklet for details about children's developmental understanding of death.*) When children express misperceptions about death, adults should always correct their misperceptions in an honest and straightforward manner. Otherwise, years later, the children might remember what they were told and feel betrayed and angry about being misled.

❏ Continue to support the crisis response team members, who need repeated thanks from their administrators and school community long after the crisis. This support should come from both the building principal and the superintendent/school board.

❏ The crisis response team members (and other local caregivers who responded to your school's crisis) need to take good care of themselves (*see Section Ten of this booklet, "Who Cares for the Caregiver?"*). Arrange for plenty of opportunities for the crisis response team to meet and process their long-term reactions to the crisis.

❏ Create an appropriate remembrance of the victims of the crisis. (*See "Cautions Regarding Memorializing" and all related points in Section Six of this booklet and, if appropriate, "Suicide Postvention" in Section Eleven for guidelines.*)

Anniversaries and Significant Dates

What You Need to KNOW

• Some specific events or time frames—called "triggers"—remind victims/survivors of the trauma they've experienced.

• "Triggering" events vary by person but may include sensing something similar to something one was aware of during the crisis; reading or seeing a news report about a similar event elsewhere; the proximity of significant family events, such as birthdays and holidays; birthdays of the deceased; involvement in the law enforcement process; involvement in the criminal justice system; and anniversaries of the event.

• "Triggering" events can bring back the emotions that occurred with the original trauma, although the intensity of the long-term reactions usually decreases over time as does the frequency of the reexperienced crisis.

What You Need to DO

Who Should Do It:
- ✔ Counseling Liaison
- ✔ Crisis Coordinator/head administrator of affected school
- ✔ Parent/Family Liaison
- ✔ All crisis response team members

❏ Prepare your school community in advance for any known triggers.

❏ If a similar crisis to one that has occurred in your school is publicized elsewhere, expect the stress reactions of your school community members to resurface or intensify. Temporarily reinstate or increase your offering of counseling services to help school community members cope.

❏ Taking positive actions after learning about a similar crisis elsewhere, such as sending sympathy cards to the victims/survivors, may make your students feel less victimized by reports of that crisis. Encourage them to take any such actions.

❏ Be aware that *any type of tragedy* that occurs in your school or community soon after a crisis will exacerbate the effects of the initial crisis for victims/survivors.

❏ Note birthdays of the deceased and allow members of your school community to commemorate them if they wish to do so.

❏ Communicate with parents about the "anniversary effect." Before any significant anniversary dates, the Parent/Family Liaison should send a note home reminding families of the significance of the date and explaining its possible "triggering" effects. The letter should detail stress reactions some parents might see in their children (or themselves and other family members) and encourage them to contact your school's counselor/psychologist for assistance if they become concerned about their children's long-term stress reactions.

❏ Mark the year anniversary of the event appropriately at school. The long-term crisis reactions of your school community (and of the surrounding community as a whole) will be more severe if the date is ignored. (*See "Modifying the Curriculum" and all points concerning memorializing victims in Section Six of this booklet for suggestions.*)

❏ Don't overlook the anniversary effects of a severe school crisis on your surrounding community. Many in your community will be strongly affected by a crisis at your school and will benefit from participating in a commemoration of the anniversary date.

❏ If your school crisis was catastrophic, ongoing assistance will likely need to continue throughout the beginning of the following school year.

twelve

When Victims or Perpetrators Return to School

What You Need to KNOW

- Welcoming the student and/or staff victims of a school crisis—particularly a violent one—back into the school community must obviously be handled with sensitivity.

- In a severe crisis in which a felony was committed, convicted student perpetrator(s) will likely not return to your school (as they will be incarcerated). Following less severe crises, you may need to coordinate the reentry of a student returning from an alternative school, juvenile detention facility, or mental health facility.

- A common strategy of schools is to transfer the student perpetrator to another campus. This strategy may help to alleviate fears in an urban school system, but it generally does not work well in a small community.

- Often a student perpetrator will move to another location or attend a private school, but those school communities, too, may be upset by the student's enrollment.

What You Need to DO

Who Should Do It:
- ✔ All crisis response team members
- ✔ Crisis Coordinator/head administrator of affected school
- ✔ Parent/Family Liaison
- ✔ Teachers

Victims

☐ Your crisis response team should meet prior to the anticipated return of injured victims to make plans to assist them.

☐ Focus on preparing their teachers to assist them with the transition, and provide staff members with the opportunity to voice their questions and concerns.

☐ Prior to the victims' return, teachers should explain to the students how to behave toward their injured classmates (i.e., they should be friendly without being overly solicitous).

☐ The Crisis Coordinator and Parent/Family Liaison should talk with victims and their families before the injured students return to school to assess their emotional state and to alleviate anxiety associated with their return. Their wishes should be accommodated whenever feasible.

☐ Encourage the parents of victims to accompany their children to school on their first day back and to stay as long as they wish.

☐ The crisis response team, school administrators, and teachers should warmly welcome the victims when they arrive at school. Communicate caring and concern, but do not embarrass the students. Take your cue from the injured students regarding the level of emotional support that is necessary or appreciated.

twelve

Student Perpetrators

❏ The Crisis Coordinator/head administrator of the affected school must stay in close contact with the prosecutor to obtain accurate information about the status of the perpetrator and provide that information to the school community. Recent legislation has made record sharing between the judicial system and schools easier.

❏ He or she should also coordinate with the staff of the facility currently housing the student to make the transition as uneventful as possible.

❏ There may be much trepidation about a convicted student perpetrator returning to school. Your crisis response team should take any and all reasonable steps to increase security and attempt to reduce the fear felt by staff and/or students.

Liability and Litigation

What You Need to KNOW

• Lawsuits against schools are becoming increasingly common as individuals vent their frustration and grief and demand significant financial damages for unsafe conditions on campus.

• Schools have also been sued for (among other things) failing to call a child protective services agency when they should have; for sexual misconduct by school employees; for personal injury and property damage to students and employees; for inappropriately disciplining students with Individualized Education Plans (IEPs); and for failing to warn parents about the suicidal intentions of their children (*see "Suicide Liability Issues" in Section Eleven of this booklet*). Schools also have a responsibility to call for medical assistance when necessary and to notify police when a serious crime occurs at school.

• The issue of school safety and the liability of educators follows a model of "reasonableness." The courts have supported the good faith efforts of schools to provide a safe and effective learning environment. Precedence indicates that for school systems/administrators to be held liable after a school crisis, they would have to have been extremely negligent and have failed to make any good faith effort to try to assist a troubled student or intervene in any preventative manner.

• School officials must act quickly in the aftermath of a crisis and they must take preventative actions when they have firsthand knowledge (or strong secondhand knowledge) of a potential crime, but they cannot be expected to read the mind of a troubled student.

twelve

continued—

What You Need to DO

Who Should Do It: ✔ Crisis Coordinator/head administrator of affected school
✔ Central office staff
✔ All crisis response team members

❏ Schools can help to protect themselves against lawsuits by developing comprehensive crisis plans and by sharing information with other professionals, agencies, and parents during a crisis. Document your crisis response activities in writing, seek guidance from your supervisor(s), and call parents whenever there is a "duty to warn" issue.

❏ After a severe school crisis, it is prudent to have your school system's attorney present at all media interviews and when any school staff members are interviewed by outside attorneys.

❏ Your school system's attorney might also wish to depose all school staff members who were involved in the crisis/the crisis response shortly after the crisis incident while the details are still fresh in their minds. Be sure your school community members have been given the opportunity to process their crisis reactions before they are deposed (*see Section Five of this booklet, "Emotional Recovery in a Crisis"*).

twelve

Key to the Checklists by Individual

Also available from Sopris West

Coping with Crisis: Lessons Learned

by Scott Poland and Jami S. McCormick

Drawn from the firsthand experiences of those "in the trenches" of crisis response, *Coping With Crisis* provides powerful crisis response recommendations that are immediately applicable—within an hour of an incident and in the days, weeks, and months that follow. Real-life case studies from two highly publicized school shootings illustrate the recommended steps to take not only in shooting incidents, but in cases of fights, bomb threats, suicides, gang-related violence, accidental deaths, and any other tragedy. Step-by-step information and ideas are offered to help schools, parents, and community caregivers:

- Aid students, families, school staff, and community members
- Manage immediate and long-term effects of crises
- Handle typical reactions to crisis, trauma, and grief
- Use a proven model to help people "process" their crisis reactions and begin emotional recovery
- Recognize suicide warning signs and provide effective postvention
- Contain, and cooperate with, the media during crises
- Guide volunteer and financial assistance
- Handle funerals and memorials, and more

To order this book or for more information, contact Sopris West at **(800) 547-6747** or visit our Web site: **www.sopriswest.com**.

SOPRIS
WEST